Greece & Rome

NEW SURVEYS IN THE CLASSICS No. 12

OVID

BY JOHN BARSBY

OXFORD
AT THE CLARENDON PRESS
1978

Oxford University Press, Walton Street, Oxford OX2 6DP
OXFORD LONDON GLASGOW
NEW YORK TORONTO MELBOURNE WELLINGTON
KUALA LUMPUR SINGAPORE JAKARTA HONG KONG TOKYO
DELHI BOMBAY CALCUTTA MADRAS KARACHI
IBADAN NAIROBI DAR ES SALAAM CAPE TOWN

ISBN 0 9030 35 08 1

Printed in Great Britain
at the University Press, Oxford
by Eric Buckley
Printer to the University

I. INTRODUCTION

This survey is, like its predecessors in the series, a 'personal synthesis' with bibliographical pointers. Ovid was the most prolific of the major Latin poets, and, in contrast to the neglect which he was still suffering in the first half of the present century,he has been the subject of an immense amount of scholarly activity over the last twenty-five years. Full bibliographies of recent work on Ovid can be found elsewhere;[1] the object of the present survey is to provide a continuous discussion of Ovid's poetry, with important bibliographical references given in the footnotes. For this purpose, a fairly rigorous process of selection has been necessary. I have in general referred only to works which are by common consent important or which I have found particularly illuminating or interesting; and even here I have preferred recent work to older,[2] work in English to that in other languages (though I hope that the main lines of non-English scholarship have been fairly represented), and readily available work to that which is less accessible or unpublished. Most of the works cited contain further bibliographical references, which will enable the reader to pursue points of interest beyond the limits of this survey.

One problem in writing a 'new survey' is to decide at what point to begin. The last major general work on Ovid in English was L. P. Wilkinson's *Ovid Recalled*, published in 1955. This sensitive and scholarly study has by no means been superseded by the researches of the last twenty years, and it would be impossible to write a new survey without echoing many of its judgements. Wilkinson's book in many ways provides the most convenient starting-point, especially as Ovid was only cursorily treated in M. Platnauer's *Fifty Years of Classical Scholarship* in 1954. Since the publication of *Ovid Recalled*, there have been few general books on Ovid, notably those of S. D'Elia (1959) and J.-M. Frécaut (1972); most of the major studies have been concerned with separate works, chiefly with the *Metamorphoses*, and these will be referred to in the relevant chapters. There have, however, been several important collections of essays since 1955; three such arose out of the bimillennial celebration of Ovid's birth in 1958 (*Ovidiana, Atti del Convegno Internazionale Ovidiano,* and *Studi Ovidiani*); and more recently there have been Ovid volumes in the

Wege der Forschung and Classical Literature and Its Influence series.

Various limitations have had to be imposed in order to keep this survey within manageable lengths. I have said little about Ovid's life and the chronology of his works,[3] less about the transmission of the text and textual problems, and nothing about Ovid's influence on later writers.[4] Nor have I attempted to discuss the lost works or the *opera incerta et minora.*[5] I have taken it that the main interest of readers will lie rather in Ovid's major poetical works and their interpretation. In this sphere some trends in modern scholarship can be fairly clearly observed. In general, the judgement of Ovid as a second-rate and superficial writer is being superseded by the idea that he is an important poet who deserves to be taken seriously. In particular, this more sympathetic approach takes three main forms—the detailed examination of Ovid's style and literary techniques (including the important question of his treatment of literary models and of the expectations of his readers),[6] the recognition of his humanity and his psychological perceptiveness, and the careful assessment of the philosophical implications of his poetry and of its relationship to its social and political context. There is always, of course, a danger of overinterpreting the past in accordance with the preconceptions of the present, and there is a temptation today to see Ovid as a psychoanalyst or as mirroring present-day uncertainties about individual identity or about the social and political structure. But there is no doubt that important and interesting questions are being posed, and that the answers given demand serious consideration in any evaluation of Ovid's achievement.

It seems best to devote a separate chapter to each of Ovid's major works, and to end this introduction with a note on chronology. The dating of the amatory works presents enormous difficulties.[7] Though the evidence for the relative dating (*Am.* 2. 18. 19 ff., *Ars* 3. 343 ff.) is full of problems, the following sequence can be accepted: *Amores* (1st edition), *Medea, Heroides* (single), *Amores* (2nd edition), *Ars Amatoria* and *Remedia Amoris, Heroides* (double). But there are very few absolute dates. Ovid began reciting his poetry in public in *c.* 25 B.C. (*Tr.* 4. 10. 57 f.); the second edition of the *Amores* was published after 16 B.C. (*Am.* 1. 14. 49); the *Ars* was finally published after 2 B.C. (*Ars* 1. 171 ff.) and the *Remedia* after A.D. 1 (*Rem.* 155 ff.). Quite how we spread Ovid's poetic activity over this period is still a matter for speculation: the surviving work has to be spread fairly thinly (8,000 lines over twenty-six years). With Ovid's later works we appear to be on firmer ground: the *Fasti, Metamorphoses*, and double *Heroides* can be dated A.D. 1–8, the *Tristia* A.D. 8–12 (with the *Ibis* soon after 8), and the *Ex Ponto* A.D. 12–16 (with some revision of the *Fasti* after A.D. 14). But the notion of the 'simultaneous' writing of such different works as the double *Heroides, Fasti*, and *Metamorphoses* presents problems, to say nothing of the combined bulk of these poems (over 18,000 lines in eight years). It is often assumed that the *Metamorphoses* was substantially written before the *Fasti*, but there is very little firm evidence.[8] It is worth remarking that the whole chronology of the pre-exile poems falls apart if the crucial passage of the *Ars* was added for the final publication (or second edition) of a work completed several years earlier; this view (now revived by no less an authority than Syme) would allow us to concentrate the amatory works into fewer years and to give more time to the composition of the *Fasti* and *Metamorphoses*.[9]

Notes
(For works cited by author's name or brief title only, see Appendix)

1. Apart from the annual reports in *APh*, see W. Kraus, *AAHG* 11 (1958), 129–46; 16 (1963), 1–14; 18 (1965), 193–208; and M. von Albrecht, *AAHG* 25 (1972), 55–76, 267–90; 26 (1973), 129–50. There is a briefly annotated bibliography in English for 1958–68 by R. J. Gariepy, *CW* 64 (1970), 37–56.

2. For the older material see E. Martini, *Einleitung zu Ovid* (Prague, 1933; repr. Darmstadt, 1970). Kraus's *RE* article (reprinted in *Wege zu Ovid*) remains fundamental. Other older discussions still worth reading include those of Rand and (especially) Fränkel.

3. On matters of biography see A. L. Wheeler, *AJPh* 46 (1925), 1–28, and Kraus (1), 67 ff.

4. This is an immense subject, of which Wilkinson's two chapters (366 ff., 399 ff.) remain the best general discussion. C. Jameson, in Binns, *Ovid*, 210 ff., gives an interesting account of Ovid in the sixteenth century. W. Stroh, *Ovid im Urteil der Nachwelt* (Darmstadt, 1969), provides an entertaining collection of verdicts on Ovid from Velleius to Pound, as well as a full bibliography for Ovid's *Nachleben* since 1935.

5. There are recent editions of the *Ibis* by A. La Penna (Florence, 1957) and J. André (Paris, 1963), and of the *Halieutica* by J. A. Richmond (London, 1962), F. Capponi (Leiden, 1972), and E. de Saint Denis (Paris, 1975). The *Ibis* can confidently be said to be Ovidian, but not the *Halieutica*, on which see J. A. Richmond, *Hermes* 96 (1968), 341–55, and *Philologus* 120 (1976), 92–106, or the *Nux*, on which see A. G. Lee, *Ovidiana*, 457–71.

6. On questions of style and literary allusion several of the older works (some recently reprinted) are still very useful. See esp. Washietl, Owen, and Wilkins on similes; Linse and Axelson on vocabulary; Zingerle, Lüneburg, and Ganzenmüller on imitation and allusion; Port on book-structure; and Platnauer on versification. The *Concordance of Ovid* by R. J. Deferrari, I. Barry, and R. P. McGuire (Washington, 1939; repr. Hildesheim, 1968) is indispensable for any study of Ovid's usage.

7. For a thorough discussion see Jacobson, 300 ff. On the first edition of *Am.* see also A. Cameron, *CQ* 18 (1968), 320–33.

8. See Fränkel, 143 and n., whose general view is still widely accepted, if not his precise dating of *Fast.* to A.D. 7–8. But Otis (2), 22, and Stössl, 22, may well be right to believe that *Fast.* was at least conceived and begun before *Met.* Ovid's claim that it was the exile that interrupted *Fast.* (*Tr.* 2. 552) need not be taken at face value.

9. In his forthcoming book *History in Ovid* Syme places the first edition of *Ars* in *c.* 8 B.C. (cf. D'Elia, 188, n. 110), and also argues that *Fast.* was broken off in A.D. 4 (I am grateful to Sir Ronald for conveying to me the essence of his views).

II. *AMORES*[1]

The most important contribution of recent scholarship to the understanding of the *Amores* is the study of Ovid's treatment of the genre and of his literary predecessors. The terms parody, travesty, and *reductio ad absurdum* are not new, but they need some further definition or amplification. What is not in doubt is that the *Amores* are basically a light-hearted reworking of the genre. They are not the product of personal emotion, nor do they have any immediate relationship to the life of the poet; and many of the questions which in the past engaged the student of love-elegy (such as morality, sincerity, autobiography) are thus unimportant or irrelevant. Some scholars still insist that Corinna was a real person;[2] but in a parody this is unlikely, and some of Ovid's own references (*Am.* 2. 17. 29 f., *Ars.* 3. 538) seem to cast doubt on her existence. This is not to say that the poet of the *Amores* was a cloistered youth whose experience of love was restricted to a study of Propertius, Tibullus, and the Greek epigram; indeed his evident understanding of the psychology of lover and mistress rather suggests the opposite.[3] But it means that the *Amores* are essentially an intellectual and literary creation, and that they depend for their effect on the co-operation of the reader, who must be thoroughly familiar with the features of the genre and be able to appreciate the subtlety and originality of Ovid's treatment.

Ovid's most evident debt is to Propertius, but it would be an oversimplification to suggest that Ovid was writing a direct parody of his elder contemporary. It is true that the Propertian lover, with his extremes of self-abnegation and self-pity, lends himself most easily to caricature; the vast majority of Ovid's poems do contain some sort of allusion to Propertius, and the structure of the final three-book edition of the *Amores* bears a strong resemblance to that of Propertius' first three books. But there are comparatively few poems in the *Amores* which are based in detail on poems of Propertius; and even here it is not usually a question of parody so much as of Ovid's taking Propertius as a starting-point for a different development of the theme or of his using the associations of the Propertius passage to highlight the irony of his own approach.[4] In any case, a study of comparable poems by the two poets invariably reveals that Ovid is drawing on much more than Propertius' treatment of the theme.[5] What Ovid is mocking—and most poems do have a note of mockery—is not Propertius but the *persona* which Ovid has himself adopted; and that *persona* is an amalgam based not only on Propertius but also on the other elegists and on the general conventions of the genre.[6] Ovid understood well the art of 'satirising the third person in terms of the first',[7] and it is one of the charms of the *Amores* that, when the lover is discomfited, we feel that Ovid is laughing at himself.

Nor is Ovid writing bare-faced travesty. In fact, the hints of irony or parody are often subtle enough for the unwary reader to be deceived, initially at least. It is only recently that the ironic undertones of 1. 3 have been fully appreciated; and interpretations which see 1. 7 as one of the most emotional poems of the collection, or which regard 3. 14 as a bitter admission by Ovid of the hollowness of his attitude to love, are misconceived.[8] It is an important part of Ovid's technique to play upon the reader's expectations.[9] Many poems are cast in the form of the dramatic monologue, in which Ovid, while addressing his mistress (or some other person), is, as it were, winking to the audience over his shoulder (as in 1. 3). At other times he will deceive the reader with a lengthy opening which disguises the real subject of the poem (1. 10), or with an unexpected ending which undercuts the apparent seriousness of what has gone before (1. 7).[10] Yet again he may confound the reader's expectations, either by the reversal of the normal behaviour of the elegiac lover (2. 19) or by the contradiction in a later poem of the attitude or situation of an earlier one (2.4 / 1. 3); or he may exceed them, by outdoing his predecessors in candour or effrontery (2. 7, 2. 8; 2. 13, 2. 14; 3. 7).

In recent years much attention has been paid to the structure of the books of the Augustan poets. The examination of the *Amores* from this point of view has not produced any very striking results. The 'programmatic' poems are duly placed (with the curious exception of 2. 18) at the beginnings and ends of books; but none of the three books has the elaborate symmetry or numerical correspondences which have been detected in Virgil's *Eclogues* or in Propertius I. It is quite reasonable to see a symmetrical structure in *Amores* I, in which the first and last poems (1 and 15) correspond, the longest poem (8) stands in the centre, and on either side of 8, the remaining poems are arranged in matching pairs (2 = 9, 3 = 10, and so on), creating a pattern of success / failure contrasts. But even this is not entirely satisfactory (it ignores the fact that 1. 11 and 1. 12 are a very closely related pair), and it is difficult to find any similar symmetry in the other two books, though the position of the Tibullus elegy (3. 9) at the centre of Book III is unlikely to be accidental. What is undeniable is that, in the three books as a whole, within the basic progression from the acceptance of elegy and love to their rejection, there is a careful concern for variety and contrast. And this is not merely a matter of aesthetics or superficial patterns: the arrangement of the poems itself, with the alternation of success and failure and of *seruitium* and *nequitia,* underlines the irony of Ovid's approach and constitutes another aspect of his playing on the reader's expectations. Notable here is the 'diptych' technique, in which the second of a pair of successive poems in some way reverses the situation of the first (1. 11 / 1. 12; 3. 11a / 3. 11b); alternatively the two contrasting poems may be separated and even occur in separate books (1. 4 / 2. 5; 2. 19 / 3. 4), which postpones the reversal and has the added effect of binding the collection together. And the imitation of the structure of Propertius I–III creates further possibilities, especially in Ovid's third book. Here the gradual inclusion of 'extraneous' poems on the Propertian model (3. 9, 3. 10, 3. 13) foreshadows a Propertian ending of the affair, but again the reader's expectations are confounded (compare Prop. 3. 24 and 3. 25 with *Am.* 3. 11 and 3. 14).[11]

There is not space in this Survey for a detailed examination of the style of the *Amores*, even though this is one of the major pleasures of the work. What can be said is that the style is eminently suitable to Ovid's general approach to elegy as outlined above; indeed the style of itself conveys the approach. Its essential characteristics are verbal and metrical dexterity; and its various features can be seen to contribute to one or more of three main effects—neatness, ingenuity, and irony. Neatness is largely a matter of antithesis, balance, and contrast, both in thought and expression, supported often by paronomasia and other kinds of verbal echoes; ingenuity is evident in word-order, brevity, compression, in allusive periphrases and in deliberate ambiguity; irony, often implied by antithesis, is enhanced by parentheses and asides.[12] The vocabulary, though inevitably based on the stock amatory vocabulary, repays careful study. Ovid coins new words in moderation, and skilfully manipulates different registers of diction against the poetic norm.[13] His echoes of non-elegiac authors, such as Virgil and Horace, amuse by the cleverness of the adaptation and the incongruousness of their new context.[14] In his handling of the elegiac couplet Ovid develops further the tendencies already visible in Tibullus. The couplet is established as a self-contained

unit, and within it the various possibilities of balance and contrast are carefully developed; at the same time the effect of lightness is increased by an unprecedented preponderance of dactyls and by the further reduction of the number of elisions. The regularization of the 3s (penthemimeral) caesura in the hexameter and (even more) of the disyllabic ending to the pentameter has been thought to create monotony, but a careful examination reveals considerable rhythmical variety in the treatment of both line and couplet.[15]
The style of the *Amores* is not, of course, beyond criticism. It is true that its brilliance is in a sense superficial, that it lacks majesty, mystery, sonority, that it is too lucid to present real intellectual problems, that its imagery tends to be commonplace (though we might admit the *desultor* metaphor at 1. 3. 15 and the stripped-cedar simile at 1. 14. 11 f. as exceptions),[16] and that (above all) the fine discipline which is applied to the individual couplet is not always applied to the poem as a whole, so that some elegies are unbalanced by the over-lengthy development of a point (1. 13, 3. 6). In fact, the characteristic Ovidian style is already established in the *Amores,* except that love-elegy does not offer much scope for developing or displaying skills in narrative or in extended description.

So far this discussion has emphasized the wit or intellectual qualities of the *Amores.* This is not to say that Ovid is lacking in humour, or that the *Amores* is an entirely superficial work. The serious note in the poems on poetic immortality (1. 15, 3. 9) has long been recognized, and modern scholars point to an underlying seriousness in Ovid's treatment of love and in his attitude to the Augustan regime. His attitude to love is of amused resignation, where the difficulties, follies, and deceptions of the lover are humorously magnified, cheerfully minimized, or positively welcomed. In a sense Ovid is offering an alternative (and perhaps more practicable) approach to love to the hopeless idealism of the other elegists and to the negative stance of the moralists (Lucr. 4. 1037 ff., Cic. *Tusc. Disp.* 4. 68 ff.).[17] The work is saved from mere triviality by the warm humanity and psychological truth which underly its ironical approach (1. 4, 1. 14); there is only one place (2. 13 and 2. 14) where Ovid's genial banter seems to descend to callousness.[18]

The technique and spirit of the *Amores* are basically Alexandrian, though in some cases (2. 16, 3. 2) the setting is clearly Roman rather than Greek. But it was impossible for a Roman of the Augustan age to detach himself from the political and social conditions of his time, and the *Amores* inevitably reflect Ovid's attitude to the regime of Augustus and its ideals. In his choice of love rather than any higher theme for poetry, and in his evident enthusiasm for the life of the lover, Ovid is clearly flying in the face of Augustus' attempts to reform marriage. In his flippant treatment of religion (3. 3) and of the military ideal (1. 9), in his equally flippant references to Augustus himself (1. 2. 51) and his buildings (2. 2. 4), and in his scorn for rustic *simplicitas* (1. 8. 39 ff.), Ovid is hinting at a position which becomes more explicit in the *Ars Amatoria*—the assertion of the validity of the life of *cultus* and modern sophistication as against the religious and moral earnestness of Augustus' reforms and his idealization of the past. But the *Amores* display indifference rather than a positive political stance. The clear tension which is observable in Propertius (2. 7) between private life and public duty is not so evident in the *Amores*; there is only one poem (1. 15) which strikes any serious note of defiance. Though some scholars have emphasized the anti-Augustan tendencies of the *Amores,* it seems better to regard the work, in intention at least, as apolitical, as un-Augustan rather than as anti-Augustan.[19]

Notes

1. Our evidence for the text of Ovid's amatory works has been augmented by the rediscovery of the manuscript Y (Hamiltonensis), once wrongly catalogued as being of the fourteenth century but now recognized as Carolingian; see F. Munari, *Il codice Hamilton 471 di Ovidio* (Rome, 1965). The standard text of the amatory works is that of E. J. Kenney (Oxford, 1961; corr. edn. 1965), on which see G. P. Goold, *HSCPh* 69 (1965), 1–107; for Kenney's subsequent remarks on Y see *CR* 16 (1966), 267–71. Goold's views on the text of *Am.* have now been incorporated into his revision of Showerman's Loeb text (London, 1914; 2nd edn. 1977). A. G. Lee's English translation (London, 1968) is a brilliant *tour de force.* The only English commentary is J. A. Barsby's on *Am.* I (Oxford, 1973); see also the editions of P. Brandt (Leipzig, 1911; repr. Hildesheim, 1963), F. Munari (Florence, 1951; 5th edn. 1970), W. Marg and R. Harder (Munich, 1957; 4th edn. 1976), and F. W. Lenz (Berlin, 1965; 3rd edn. 1976). Apart from the relevant chapters of Fränkel, Wilkinson, D'Elia, and Frécaut (reference to which is assumed in each chapter of this Survey) there are good recent discussions of *Am.* by Lee and Du Quesnay; see also Reitzenstein, Otis (1), and Marg. There is a bibliography for *Am.* in Munari's edition (xxxix ff., 221 ff.) and for the amatory works as a whole in Zinn, 110 ff.

2. e.g. de Saint Denis, 185 ff., and P. Green, *Essays in Antiquity* (London, 1960), 118 ff. On the whole question see J. P. Sullivan, *TAPhA* 92 (1961), 522 ff., and Williams, 538 ff.

3. On the relationship between life and literature in Roman personal poetry see J. P. Sullivan, *Arion* 1:3 (1962), 34 f.; G. Williams, *Horace* (Oxford, 1972), 1 f.; and Rudd, 145 ff. The pendulum is swinging away from the over-rigid application of the *persona* theory, especially for poets like Propertius and Horace; it remains essentially valid for Ovid.

4. On Ovid's use of Propertius see K. Morgan, *Ovid's Art of Imitation: Propertius in the Amores* (Leiden, 1977); cf. K. Berman, *CPh* 67 (1972), 170–7. R. Neumann, *Qua Ratione Ovidius in Amoribus Scribendis Properti Elegiis Usus Sit* (Diss. Göttingen, 1919), is still useful for his compilation of parallels; see also Zingerle, i. 109 ff., and Ganzenmüller, 292 ff.

5. See e.g. F. O. Copley, *Exclusus Amator* (Baltimore, 1956), 113 ff., on *Am.* 1. 6 and Prop. 1. 16; K. Quinn, *Latin Explorations* (London, 1963), 239 ff., on *Am.* 2. 11

and Prop. 1. 8; and E. Courtney, *BICS* 16 (1969), 80 ff., on *Am.* 1. 8 and Prop. 4. 5.

6. On Ovid's relation to earlier elegy and its Greek sources see A. A. Day, *The Origins of Latin Love Elegy* (Oxford, 1938; repr. Hildesheim, 1972) and G. Luck, *The Latin Love Elegy* (London, 1959; 2nd edn. 1969). For his echoes of Catullus and Tibullus see Zingerle, i. 35 ff., 54 ff., and Ganzenmüller, 279 ff. On his adaptation of the Callimachean *apologia* see Wimmel, 295 ff.; for his burlesque of the 'usefulness of poetry to win one's mistress' theme see Stroh, 141 ff.

7. See Rand, 12.

8. On 1. 3 see L. C. Curran, *CPh* 61 (1966), 47–9; on 1. 7 see H. A. Khan, *Latomus* 25 (1966), 880–94 (cf. Fränkel, 17 ff.); on 3. 14 see A. G. Lee, *Gnomon* 32 (1960), 518 (cf. F. W. Lenz, *SIFC* 12 (1935), 227–35; Fränkel, 30 f.; and Luck, *The Latin Love Elegy*, 173 ff.).

9. See P. J. Connor, *Ramus* 3 (1974), 18–40.

10. On the Ovidian coda see D. Parker, *Arion* 8 (1969), 80–97.

11. On structure see Marg, 302 ff.; Williams, 514 ff.; and especially G. Lörcher, *Der Aufbau der drei Bücher von Ovids Amores* (Amsterdam, 1975).

12. On these aspects of Ovid's style see Frécaut, 25–171.

13. R. Pichon, *Index Verborum Amatoriorum* (Paris, 1902; repr. Hildesheim, 1966), provides a convenient guide to the vocabulary of the elegists. D. Donnet, *LEC* 33 (1965), 253–79, shows that Ovid makes much less use of 'emotional' words than the other elegists. On new coinages see Linse; on registers of vocabulary see in general Axelson, and for an example L. C. Curran, *Phoenix* 18 (1964), 314–19, on 1. 10.

14. For echoes of Horace see Zingerle, iii. 9 ff.; for echoes of Virgil see Zingerle, ii. 48 ff., and Döpp, 13 ff.

15. On metrical matters see Platnauer and Wilkinson, 27 ff. H. Drexler, *Philologus* 109 (1965), 219–45, demonstrates the variety of possible pentameter patterns.

16. On similes see Washietl, Owen, and Wilkins.

17. So Du Quesnay, 42. See also the interesting discussion by Frécaut, 183 ff.

18. On the abortion poems see W. J. Watts, *AClass* 16 (1973), 89–101.

19. On the politics of elegy see J. P. Sullivan, *Arethusa* 5 (1972), 17–34; on 1. 15 see F. Stössl in *Festschrift Karl Vretska* (Heidelberg, 1970), 250–75.

III. *HEROIDES*[1]

The question of authenticity still exercises scholars; one recent critic has even reduced the number of genuine *Heroides* to ten (namely 1–7, 10, 11, and 15).[2] The poems chiefly under suspicion are 9 (Deianira), 15 (Sappho), and 16–21 (the double letters). The most cogent arguments against 9 and 16–21 are the metrical ones, but for the double letters these diminish with the later dating. The Sappho letter (15) has been transmitted separately from the rest of the *Heroides*; it may be that it was deliberately omitted because of its anomalous (non-mythological) subject-matter when the single and double letters were united into one collection, but there are still some linguistic oddities which need explaining.[3] For the purpose of this discussion I have assumed that all twenty-one of the *Heroides* are genuine; I have also chosen to discuss the work as a single collection rather than as two separate ones.[4]

One of the important tendencies of recent work on the *Heroides* is the questioning of the commonly held ideas that the poems are merely rhetorical exercises and that the collection as a whole is monotonous. The charge has frequently been made that the *Heroides* are simply versified *suasoriae*, but a careful examination of the question shows that the letters of Ovid's heroines (Phaedra's is a possible exception) have little in common with the practice of the *suasoria* as we know it from the elder Seneca. They bear still less relation to the *controuersia*, for which Ovid even as a student of rhetoric had little liking (Sen. *Contr.* 2. 2. 12). And, if they do owe something to the school exercise of *ethopoeia* or *prosopopoeia* (and it is worth reminding ourselves that the only examples which we have of these *progymnasmata* for comparison come from a period two centuries after Ovid), this is no ground for condemnation; it is no discredit to a writer to have had some formal training in the techniques of his art.[5] Nor does it detract from Ovid's claim of originality for the *Heroides* as a literary genre (*Ars* 3. 346). The idea of a poetic love-epistle may well have been suggested by Propertius 4. 3, but the differences between this and the *Heroides* need to be stressed. As for Hellenistic precedents, no clear evidence of Hellenistic verse love-letters has been found, and, even if Ovid was aware of and used the precepts of Hellenistic prose epistolography, this again does nothing to diminish the novelty of the *Heroides*.[6]

The charge of monotony is a more serious one. Ovid must have been aware of the danger; indeed, it is more than likely that in inventing the genre he was deliberately setting himself the artistic challenge of creating variety within a circumscribed field. Here it must be emphasized that a genre can scarcely exist without a standard language and stock themes, nor can the technique of *uariatio* be practised without them; it is they that set up expectations in the reader, which the author can then manipulate to his own and the reader's pleasure. The differences in the external circumstances of the various heroines are not in dispute: the situations of Penelope, Briseis, Phaedra, Hermione, Canace, Laodamia, and Hypermnestra have little in common with each other, or with the 'stock' situation as represented by Phyllis or Ariadne. It is often said, for example, that the heroines all speak the same (Ovidian) language, but careful examination shows greater variety than is at first apparent. Oenone has a propensity for images from nature, Canace avoids extreme flights of rhetoric, Hypermnestra rarely surmounts the barrier of the end-stopped line, and Sappho's language is tinged with echoes from her own poetry.[7] The stock themes also are skilfully varied. An obvious example is the child motif (Dido is, or may be, merely pregnant; Canace's child has been killed; Hypsipyle plans to confront Jason with his unknown twins; Medea uses Jason's known and beloved children to persuade him); other themes are varied in rather more subtle ways, the departure scene, for example.[8] A further form of variation is in the structure of the different poems. The two main ingredients, narrative and argument, are mixed in various ways and in various proportions: Canace has almost entirely narrative, Penelope virtually none. Again, some poems have clear dramatic movement or psychological progression (Deianira, Medea), others are comparatively static (Penelope, Dido).[9] So the single letters have considerable variation, if we are prepared to look for it, and indeed to appreciate it as something of a *tour de force.* And the double letters carry this variation still further, by focusing part of the attention on the male lover, by picking up the love affair at an earlier stage where the woman still has some room for manœuvre, and by introducing a strong element of confrontation and interaction between the two partners. Moreover, the double letters not only differ from the single ones in these respects, but are also very different from each other in character and situation and in tone and style.[10]

The question of variation in character between heroines is bound up with the question of Ovid's psychological perception. This has been variously estimated; it is not doubted that Ovid shows unusual sympathy with and understanding of the female point of view, but this of itself neither makes him a psychologist nor ensures that the different female characters have any individuality. Some critics have sought out the 'psychopathology' of each of the heroines and come up with a series of sharply differentiated characters; this line of criticism has been taken to unacceptable extremes, but it does make it clear that the *Heroides* are not simply a series of stereotypes. It can be asserted that in many cases love is not the only or even the dominant emotion, and that Ovid is concerned to explore other aspects of personality. Two examples must suffice. Briseis is not just a lovesick captive woman deprived of her lover, but a princess, who having lost home and family in the war is now utterly dependent on Achilles for her future security; her dominant emotion is fear rather than love. Hermione is not merely a girl married to a man she dislikes rather than the one she loves; she is the victim of an emotional insecurity stemming from her childhood longings and separation from her mother. These are two women of very different kinds, but in both cases Ovid has deliberately emphasized an aspect of their past to give greater depth to his portrayal of their present behaviour. It is this sort of treatment which makes Ovid something of a psychologist as well as a feminist, and which gives to each of the heroines a distinct identity of her own.[11]

Another ramification of the same question is that of Ovid's treatment of earlier versions of the various myths. Unfortunately, in most cases his sources are either unknown or fragmentary, so that we cannot share the expectations of Ovid's original readers or fully appreciate the skill of his adaptations.[12] But from those letters where he can reasonably be assumed to have used a single still extant source we can form some idea of his general approach. It seems that essentially his aim was to revitalize the myth by approaching it from a new perspective and giving it a new psychological realism. The Briseis letter is a good example, an ingenious reconstruction of the relevant parts of the *Iliad* from an entirely new angle and at the same time a convincing psychological study. The Dido episode is divested of the higher significance that it had in the context of the *Aeneid,* and becomes instead a study in more modern terms of the feelings of a woman deserted by her lover in these particular circumstances. In the case of Acontius and Cydippe, though we have Callimachus' version only in fragmentary form, it seems clear that Ovid has again given a new psychological depth to his portrayal of the two characters, while at the same time exploiting the legal aspects of the situation in Roman terms. But in most cases we cannot now trace the complexity of Ovid's adaptations with any certainty; it is possible, for example, that his Phyllis was created by a kind of *contaminatio* with Virgil's Dido, and that his Dido owes something to Catullus' Ariadne.[13]

One of the problems of the *Heroides* is Ovid's failure to maintain any consistency of tone. It is undeniable that there are passages of lyrical beauty in the work, especially in the narrative passages, and passages of genuine pathos, but it worries critics that neither the lyricism nor the pathos is maintained for long.[14] The culprit is usually seen to be Ovid's style, with its strong rhetorical, intellectual, and even mischievous qualities; and it is true that the style which was eminently suited to the *Amores,* where the essence of the approach was wit and where exaggerations of style were part of the irony, is not well suited to the serious portrayal of feeling. In the *Heroides* the various strokes of the verbal wit, though sometimes appropriate to the character of the speaker,[15] often seem out of place. The effect is to transfer the attention from the heroine to Ovid himself, with the inevitable 'distancing' effect on the reader. Equally distracting is Ovid's treatment of the letter form, not disguising its limitations but using them to amuse the reader—hence the opening epistolary conceits, hence the deliberate acknowledgement of the implausibility of the letter-writing situation (1. 59 ff., 4. 3 ff.), hence the startling dramatic development which occurs 'during the course of writing' at 9. 143, all of which by their obtrusiveness distract from the serious consideration of the plight of the heroine.[16] But it would be obtuse to insist that the real aim of the *Heroides* was to portray genuine feeling and then to complain that the unsuitability of the style prevents this aim being achieved; better to take the view that the essence of the work is the wit, the rhetoric, and the irony, and to add that these do not preclude the occasional moment of lyricism or pathos or the expression of valid insights into human behaviour.[17]

As with the *Amores,* there is something to be gained by looking at the *Heroides* not as a collection of separate poems, but as a corpus with its own deliberate echoes, contrasts, and cross-references. Nothing much emerges from the attempt to find a fixed scheme or pattern in the order of the poems, though there is a clear tendency to separate poems involving the same characters (6, 12) or similar situations (2, 6, 10).[18] The collection is unified by the repetition of stock themes, by the reappearance of the same characters (Jason twice, Helen four times), and by the recurrence of the same basic myth (the Trojan War is the subject of eight of the letters); and the genealogical connections between the various characters (Demophoon and Theseus, Hypsipyle and

Ariadne) are emphasized by the propensity of the heroines to recall the ancestry of themselves and their lovers. This interrelationship between the different epistles creates possibilities of irony, as when Medea, once the object of Hypsipyle's jealousy, finds herself echoing many of Hypsipyle's arguments when herself abandoned. More interestingly, it creates a series of different perspectives, whereby a myth is no longer told as a coherent whole but seen from a number of partial and egocentric viewpoints. Thus it is possible to suggest that the *Heroides*, while they make no explicit statement, imply a profound comment on the subjectivity of truth or on the capacity of the individual for self-deception.[19]

If we are to seek profundity beneath the wit and rhetoric of the *Heroides*, it is likely to lie in these areas of perspective and (more so) in the sympathetic psychology of Ovid's characterization. It is harder to justify the view that the work makes any real comment on the contemporary political situation. It is true that the Paris–Helen letters are very reminiscent of the tone of the *Ars Amatoria*, and that Phaedra's is an invitation to adultery showing the same scorn for *uetus pietas* (4. 131) as does the bawd of the *Amores*. But the work as a whole can scarcely be said to be subversive of the ideal of marriage: male infidelity, for instance, is not portrayed in a favourable light. Nor is it reasonable to see the Dido epistle as a direct attack on the *Aeneid* (or on the traditional characterization of Aeneas) and thus implicitly on Augustan values. The *Heroides*, like the *Amores*, are surely un-Augustan rather than anti-Augustan.[20]

The *Heroides* represent an advance in Ovid's development over the *Amores* in two ways (which is not to say that they are therefore a more successful work). Though based on the elegiac theme of separation from the beloved, they move from the limited situations of the elegiac lover to the broader world of mythology, where there is a wider range of situations and characters and greater opportunity for drama and pathos. At the same time they represent an advance in Ovid's treatment of myth. In love-elegy, myth is merely a source of *exempla* (which Ovid often uses mischievously); in the *Heroides* it becomes a subject for poetry in its own right but with a new humanizing and modernizing slant. In this way the *Heroides* represent Ovid's first attempt to revitalize mythology, and thus look forward to the *Metamorphoses*.

Notes

1. Our understanding of the manuscript tradition of *Her.* has been greatly advanced by H. Dörrie, *Untersuchungen zur Überlieferungsgeschichte von Ovids Epistulae Heroidum*

(Göttingen, i and ii 1960, iii 1972). However, both Dörrie's own text (Berlin, 1971) and that of R. Giomini (Rome, i 1957, 2nd edn. 1963, ii 1965) are disappointing; the best plain text is now G. P. Goold's thorough revision of the Loeb edition (London, 1977). There are no good modern English translations; H. C. Cannon's version in heroic couplets (New York, 1971) is undistinguished. Apart from Dörrie's commentary, that of A. Palmer (Oxford, 1898; repr. Hildesheim, 1967) is still very useful. We now have two good critical discussions, both confined to the single letters, by Oppel and Jacobson, which are fundamental to the literary appreciation of the work; see also the shorter accounts of Kraus (2), Dörrie, and Anderson. There is a comprehensive bibliography in Dörrie's edition, 19 ff. and after each letter.

2. So G. P. Goold, *Gnomon* 46 (1974), 484.

3. On *Her.* 9 see D. W. T. C. Vessey, *CQ* 19 (1969), 349–61, whose statistics for 4w hexameter caesuras and for spondaic pentameter openings deserve respect (his other arguments are countered by Jacobson, 228 ff.). On *Her.* 16–21 E. Courtney, *BICS* 12 (1965), 63–6, has revived and amplified the metrical objections, but the careful analysis of S. B. Clark, *HSCPh* 19 (1908), 121–55, is still persuasive; V. A. Tracy, *CJ* 66 (1971), 328–30, has shown that the diction of the double letters is thoroughly Ovidian; for other arguments in favour of authenticity see Kraus (2). On *Her.* 15 we now have the extensive monograph of H. Dörrie, *P. Ovidius Naso: der Brief der Sappho an Phaon* (Munich, 1975), who accepts the genuineness of the letter, as does Jacobson, 277 f.; on the transmission see also A. R. Baca, *TAPhA* 102 (1971), 29–38.

4. On the dating of the single letters see Jacobson, 300 ff., who puts them in the period 10–3 B.C. The double letters belong to the period A.D. 1–8; see Kraus (2), 294.

5. On the relationship of *Her.* to the *suasoria* and *controuersia* see Oppel, 37 ff., 68 ff. (cf. Fränkel, 36 and n.); on *ethopoeia* see Jacobson, 325 ff. Ovid's debt to rhetoric in general is minimized by R. F. Higham, *Ovidiana*, 32–48.

6. On Prop. 4. 3 see Dörrie, 50 f., and H. Merklin, *Hermes* 96 (1968), 461–94; on epistolography see L. Winniczuk, *Publius Ovidius Naso* (Bucharest, 1957), 39–70, and Jacobson, 331 ff.

7. So Jacobson, 135 f., 168 ff., 191 f., 280 ff.; see also E. M. Bradley, *CJ* 44 (1969), 158–62, on Oenone, and M. Treu, *PP* 8 (1953), 356–64, on Sappho.

8. See Jacobson, 381 ff.

9. See Jacobson, 363 ff.; Oppel, 10 ff., has a useful formal analysis of each epistle.

10. See the discussions of Kraus (2), 278 ff., Anderson, 68 ff., and Frécaut, 206 ff.

11. On Ovid's psychology see Oppel, 95 ff., and Jacobson, 371 ff. and *passim*. Jacobson illustrates well the possibilities, and the dangers, of the psychoanalytical approach.

12. Jacobson has a thorough discussion of the sources for each of the single epistles, but with few positive results.

13. On *Her.* 3 see Jacobson, 12 ff., and Wilkinson, 89 ff. (Jacobson gives the letter more psychological depth). On *Her.* 7 Jacobson, 76 ff., supports Wilkinson's unfavourable verdict (92 f.), but other scholars have been more sympathetic, notably A. G. Lee, *Atti* ii. 408, Döpp, 26 ff., and Anderson, 49 ff. On *Her.* 20 and 21 see M. L. Coletti, *RCCM* 4 (1962), 294–303, and E. J. Kenney, *Arion* 9 (1970), 388–414. On *contaminatio* see Döpp, 18 ff., 51 ff.

14. For examples of lyricism and pathos see Wilkinson, 99 ff., and A. Salvatore, *Atti* ii. 235–56.

15. For some examples, not all equally convincing, see Frécaut, 203 f.

16. On the epistolary form, and on the related question of the authenticity of the opening couplets, see E.-A. Kirfel, *Untersuchungen zur Briefform der Heroides Ovids* (Bern, 1969).

17. We lack a sympathetic discussion of the style of *Her.* E. Cappechi, *SIFC* 39 (1967), 67–111, and 41 (1969), 95–127, reaches negative conclusions on the effectiveness of Ovid's alliteration and other forms of word-play.

18. See Jacobson, 407 ff. Dörrie, 45, sees a basic alternation in *Her.* 1–15 between heroines who survive and those who die as a result of their love.

19. On 'the role of perspective' see Jacobson, 349 ff.

20. For the anti-Augustan view see Jacobson, 7, 90, 354.

IV. *ARS AMATORIA* AND *REMEDIA AMORIS*[1]

If the *Heroides* are an adaptation of the elegiac tradition to the epistolary form, then the *Ars* and *Remedia* are an adaptation to the didactic, with the crucial difference that, unlike the poetic epistle, the didactic poem had a clearly defined tradition and (in Virgil) a distinguished recent practitioner. The Hesiodic tradition had been enlarged by the Alexandrians to include the learned scientific, and had more recently been debased by the inclusion of the trivial (*Tr.* 2. 471 ff.), and it is important to see where Ovid stands. Superficially, the *Ars Amatoria* is on a par with practical poems like that of Ovid's contemporary Grattius on hunting, and the *Remedia Amoris* has affinities with medical works like Macer's on the cures for snake-bites; but the use of the didactic form for such an untraditional subject as love creates 'a pleasing atmosphere of burlesque'.[2] Ovid establishes his place in the higher poetic form of the tradition by using the standard introductory (*principio*), transitional (*adde quod*), and hortatory (*accipe*) formulae of Lucretius and Virgil and by employing the traditional ship and chariot metaphors for the progress of the poem.[3] But the *Ars* lacks the dedication to a patron which is common in more serious works, and the proem, in which Ovid denies the traditional divine inspiration (1. 25) and claims that his poem is entirely based on *usus* (1. 29), announces his ironical approach to the genre. When Ovid refers to his literary predecessors, it is in no spirit of reverence, but in order to show how cleverly he can twist their serious themes to his own light-hearted purpose; thus Lucretius' birth of civilization passage is adapted to prove the susceptibility of women to love (2. 467 ff.), and Virgil's instructions to observe the seasons and the different types of soil become with a little modification instructions on how to find and win women (1. 399 ff., 755 ff.). It is possible too that Ovid makes similar use of didactic works in prose; many scholars have seen in the structure of Book I of the *Ars* a parody of the structure of some *ars oratoria* (*inuentio* = how to find the girl, and so on).[4] But Ovid's most interesting adaptation of the genre is his creation of a humorous *persona* for the *praeceptor amoris,* thus underlining the element of burlesque. This *persona* makes extravagant claims for his powers, seeing himself as an Automedon who controls the chariot of Love or as a

Chiron or Calchas (1. 5 ff., 2. 735 ff.) and boasting that he could have saved Medea or Ariadne from their fates (3. 33 ff.); this pretentiousness is then undercut by admissions that he is on occasion at a loss (*Rem.* 577 f.) or is betraying his own interests (3. 667 ff.) or is unable to carry out his precepts in his own life (2. 547 ff.). Thus between the sophisticated poet and his sophisticated readers, we have the fictitious *praeceptor* and the equally fictitious pupils to whom the work is ostensibly addressed. In other words, the whole thing is an elaborate literary game.[5]

It is obvious enough that the *Ars* and *Remedia* make extensive use of the themes of love-elegy. It is also clear that love-elegy already possessed a strong didactic element, which needed little adaptation to fit into a didactic poem.[6] Two questions are worth asking. The first is how far Ovid has transformed the elegiac attitude to love in making it a subject for didactic poetry. The traditional *furor* of the lover is scarcely susceptible to control by *ars*; Ovid specifically claims to have replaced *impetus* by *ratio* (*Rem.* 10), and indeed the whole of the *Ars* depends on treating love as a game based on pretence and deception rather than on genuine emotion. The only concession to genuine feeling is the admission that pretence may lead to the real thing, which is explicitly stated in the *Ars* (1. 615 ff.) and is implied by the need for a *Remedia.* All this is a long way from Propertius and Tibullus; it is not so far from the *Amores,* where, though it suits Ovid's purpose to maintain the idea of love as a *furor*, the lover in practice often behaves in a detached and calculating way, treating the affair as a game rather than an affliction and showing the same readiness to admit deceptions. In other words, the essential transformation of the elegiac attitude to love had already been made in the *Amores.*[7] The second question is how much repetition the stock themes of elegy can bear before they become monotonous. In some cases a successful treatment in elegy loses its freshness and effect when repeated in the *Ars*; an obvious example is the circus flirtation (*Ars* 1. 135 ff. / *Am.* 3. 2), though the *Ars* version is of more merit than critics have sometimes been willing to allow. There are also many examples where a stock theme of elegy is adapted as didactic for *Ars* I and II, modified for the female point of view in *Ars* III, and then reversed for the *Remedia*; and even Ovid himself seems to admit that the process is in danger of becoming monotonous (3. 748, *Rem.* 811). In fact, the success of the reprise depends in each case on the wit of its presentation, which needs to be carefully studied; in this respect the *Remedia*, with its opportunities for neat reversals, comes off better than *Ars* III. And a statistical check on the amount of repetition is useful: even in the *Remedia,* which comes (as it were) at the end of the line, only two-fifths of the precepts are in fact inversions of those given earlier.[8]

One essential difference between the *Ars* and *Remedia* and the *Heroides* and *Amores* is that the two didactic poems are unmistakably set in contemporary Rome. The *Heroides* are set in the world of mythology, and the *Amores* in the shadowy half-Roman half-Hellenistic world of elegy. The contemporary element of the *Ars* and *Remedia* has two aspects. One is that they afford many delightful glimpses of the more private aspects of Roman life.[9] The other is that they can hardly avoid making at least an implicit comment on Augustan society and on the ideals of the regime; the ideas that were hinted at in the *Amores* now come over much more strongly. The most striking passage is 3. 113 ff., where Ovid explicitly rejects the idealization of the past and of rustic simplicity in favour of the splendour of contemporary Rome and the life of *cultus*. In this he is of course running contrary to the spirit of the *Georgics*; and some scholars argue that Ovid's references to the *Georgics* in these two poems are not merely part of a claim to be writing in the didactic tradition, but are a deliberate parody of the ideals and patriotism of Virgil's poem.[10] However this may be, the main theme of the *Ars,* a manual of seduction and intrigue, is clearly in conflict with Augustus' attempts to encourage marriage (2. 155); and Ovid's claims not to be writing for married women (1. 31 ff.) do nothing to disguise this fact. And there are various other ways in which Ovid seems to show little respect for Augustus and for the symbols of his prestige. His building programme (1. 71 ff.), his public spectacles (1. 171 ff.), his foreign policy (1. 177 ff.), and his cults of the gods (1. 637 ff.) are all either treated frivolously or at least debased by being set in a frivolous context. All this does not turn Ovid into a political pamphleteer or imply that the main purpose of the *Ars* and *Remedia* was to criticize Augustus and his regime. What is clear is that Ovid's natural impudence, irreverence, and sense of the incongruous (evident, for example, in his treatment of myth)[11] were not inhibited by any feeling of veneration for the ideals of Augustus or for the poetry of Virgil (1. 453). He no doubt expected to delight many of his readers by his daring, and he was not concerned if he shocked others. He himself brushed off criticisms of the *Ars* with an airy confidence (*Rem.* 359 ff.), and in this he ultimately miscalculated. In the end a jaundiced officialdom seized upon the subversive aspects of the work, but its original purpose was surely humorous rather than political.[12]

The examination of the structure of the individual books of the

Ars and *Remedia* has not produced any striking or conclusive results. Ovid has left us very few positive indications, apart from the division of *Ars* I into finding and winning the girl (1. 263 ff.); of the other apparent clues, the various metaphorical references to an inner course (2. 426, 3. 467, *Rem.* 397) merely signify returns from digressions, and the *parua / maiora* distinction which seems to coincide with a genuine subdivision at 3. 499 does not do so at 2. 535. It is reasonable to see a twofold division of the precepts of *Ars* III (catching the man and keeping him), corresponding to the division between *Ars* I and II, and to divide the first half of this into three main sections (appearance, accomplishments, and making contact); but there does not seem to be a clear plan for *Ars* II or the *Remedia.*[13] A more interesting question is the structure of the four books taken as a whole. It is clear that *Ars* I and II were originally planned as a two-book entity (1. 35 ff.) and that *Ars* III and the *Remedia* were later additions. Ovid has made some attempt to link the four books together formally by cross-references in their prologues and epilogues, though he evidently did not think it worth while to obliterate the traces of the original two-book plan. But in fact the whole adds up to a four-book unity, since the *Remedia* is a logical sequence to the *Ars,* written in exactly the same spirit and bound to it by echoes of theme and imagery; indeed the progression from *Ars* to *Remedia* exactly mirrors the progression from love to disillusionment evident in collections of love-elegies such as Propertius I–III or *Amores* I–III.[14]

The basic style of the *Ars* and *Remedia* is the style of the *Amores,* characterized by its neatness and wit. This style, which was in danger of seeming incongruous in the mouths of the speakers of the *Heroides,* is perfectly suited to the *persona* of the *praeceptor amoris.* The most significant stylistic developments in the *Ars* and *Remedia* (apart from the adoption of didactic formulae and imagery) are in the techniques of description and narrative, evident especially in the vignettes of Roman life and in the set-piece mythological digressions. A careful analysis of the language of the descriptive passages (both of city-life and in the many similes from nature) reveals an eye for detail and a sense of colour and brightness, vigour and enjoyment, beauty and elegance.[15] The narratives have many qualities, the essential difference from the first-person *Heroides* narratives being that the personality of the poet-narrator can now be allowed to obtrude. As an example, the Rape of the Sabines episode (1. 89 ff.) includes the following features: aphorism, word-play, verbal repetition, antithesis; extended description, with small details and hints of colour and scent; similes from nature;

vivid narrative, with apostrophe, focus on individuals, and short passages of direct speech; carefully varied rhythms, with a periodic four-line sentence to build up suspense and a passage of a very short clauses for the climax; editorial parenthesis and comment; impudent reinterpretation of Roman history; aetiological conclusion.[16] Other passages have greater sense of incongruity (Pasiphae) or more pictorial detail (Ariadne) or more pathos (Phyllis); but here undeniably is the basis of the narrative style of the *Fasti* and (with the change to the hexameter medium) of the *Metamorphoses.*

The final question is whether the *Ars* and *Remedia* are anything more than a *jeu d'esprit.* It is no doubt right to emphasize that the main quality of these poems is wit, and that their main appeal lies in their sophistication and ingenuity. However, like the *Amores,* they are saved from triviality or mere frivolity by their underlying humanity and psychological insight. It has often been observed that Ovid draws on works of serious philosophy in framing his precepts: the instructions to women in *Ars* III share certain principles with Cicero, *De Officiis* 1. 128 ff., and the advice in the *Remedia* echoes that of Cicero, *Tusculan Disputations* 4. 74 f. and Lucretius 4. 1058 ff. Further, the instructions on how to keep a woman's favour in *Ars* II have elements in common with the advice to legacy-hunters in Horace, *Satires* 2. 5 (and satire, for all its humorous aspects, is based on an understanding of human behaviour).[17] The aim of these borrowings may partly have been to show how cleverly Ovid could adapt other works to his own purposes, but the passages do not read like parody, and the effect is to give a backbone of human understanding to the poems. There are certainly many instances of psychological acuteness;[18] and, though a recent commentator has found few traces of 'genuine kindness', the older scholars were surely right to emphasize the basic decency with which the game of seduction and deception was to be played, and to argue that in setting up *cultus* as an ideal of civilized life Ovid was not being entirely frivolous.[19]

Notes

1. The standard text of *Ars* and *Rem.* is that of E. J. Kenney (Oxford, 1961; corr. edn. 1965); F. W. Lenz's two Paravia editions (*Ars*: Turin, 1969; *Rem.*: Turin, 1965) have more extensive *apparatus* and include the readings of Y. There are two recent English translations of *Ars* and *Rem.*, both of some merit, P. Turner's in prose (London, 1968) and R. Humphries's in verse (Bloomington, 1957). The only commentary in English is that of A. S. Hollis on *Ars* I (Oxford, 1977); see also the German editions of Lenz (*Ars*: Berlin, 1969; *Rem.*: Berlin, 1960, 2nd edn. 1968) and P. Brandt (Leipzig, 1902; repr. Hildesheim, 1963). Among recent general discussions are those by de Saint Denis, 190 ff., and Hollis. There is a bibliography for *Ars* and *Rem.* (together with *Am.* and *Her.*) in Zinn, 110 ff.

2. So Wilkinson, 120. On Ovid's relation to the didactic tradition see E. Pöhlmann, *Aufstieg und Niedergang der römischen Welt* i. 3 (Berlin, 1973), 859 ff.; cf. J. Krokowski, *Eos* 53 (1963), 143–56. For the possibility that Ovid may have used Grattius or some similar *ars uenatoria* for the hunting imagery in *Ars* see Krokowski, 152 ff., and Leach, 144 f.

3. See Kenney (1), 201 ff.

4. There is a good discussion of Ovid's use of *Geo.* by Leach; see also Kenney (1); Döpp, 95 ff.; and Rudd, 19 ff. On his use of an *ars oratoria* see T. Zielinski, *Philologus* 64 (1905), 1–26, followed by D'Elia, 178 f.; but the resemblances may be illusory.

5. On Ovid's *persona* see R. M. Durling, *CJ* 53 (1958), 157–67; cf. J. M. Fyler, *CJ* 66 (1971), 196–203.

6. See A. L. Wheeler, *CPh* 5 (1910), 440–50, and 6 (1911), 56–77, who also pursues the Greek sources.

7. See Hollis, 93 ff.

8. On the circus episode see E. Thomas, *Hommages à M. Renard* (Brussels, 1969), i. 710–24, and K. Jäger in Zinn, 51–60, as against the negative verdict of Wilkinson, 143 For some other repeated themes see Hollis, 100 ff. Opinions of *Ars* III and *Rem.* differ. Against Hollis's favourable verdict on *Rem.* (110 ff.) should be set the criticisms of D'Elia, 216 ff., who also underlines the deficiencies of *Ars* III. The proportion of reversals in *Rem.* (in fact 16 out of 42) was established by K. Prinz, *WSt* 36 (1914), 36–83, and 39 (1917), 91–121, 259–90, which remains an important study.

9. These are well illustrated by Wilkinson, 140 ff., and D'Elia, 198 ff.

10. See Kenney (1), 208, and Leach, 154.

11. See de Saint Denis, 194 ff.

12. See the excellent discussion by Rudd, 1 ff.; Hollis, 85 ff., reaches essentially the same conclusion.

13. On structure see the essays in Zinn's collection. On *Ars* III A. Hermann (29 ff.) agrees in many points with Fränkel, 205 f. For *Rem.* T. Greiner's proposed tripartite division (35 ff.) is preferable to K. Weisert's 'four pentads' (4 ff.). In general the more complex the proposed scheme the less conviction it carries.

14. So Pöhlmann, *Aufstieg und Niedergang* i. 3. 892 ff.; see also Frécaut, 235. The old idea that *Rem.* was a recantation can now be decently laid to rest.

15. See D'Elia, 198 ff.

16. On the reinterpretation of history in this episode see A. E. Wardman, *CQ* 15 (1965), 101–3; on metre and rhythm in *Ars* see D'Elia, 207 f.; on similes see the classifications of Washietl and Wilkins and the statistics of Owen (99 f.), who shows that similes are much more frequent in *Ars* (one in 38.2 lines) than in *Her.* (one in 73.3) or in *Am.* (one in 64.6).

17. Many of the parallels between Cicero and Ovid listed in C. Atzert's Teubner edition of Cic. *De Off.* (Leipzig, 1949), xxxii f., seem to be negated by the complete difference of context in *Ars*, but Ovid does follow Cicero's principle of *decorum* and echo some of his details; see also Kenney (1), 206 f., and S. D'Elia, *Atti del 1. congresso internazionale di studi Ciceroniani* (Rome, 1961), ii. 127–40. On Ovid and Hor. *Sat.* 2. 5 see D'Elia, *Ovidio,* 179 ff.

18. For examples see Wilkinson, 134 ff., and D'Elia, 224 ff.

19. The quotation is from Hollis (on 1. 767 ff.). On decency see Rand, 42 ff.; Fränkel, 57 ff.; Kraus (1), 101 f.; Frécaut, 220 ff. On *cultus* see Kraus (1), 101, and D'Elia, 188 ff.

V. *FASTI*[1]

The *Fasti* has often been regarded as one of Ovid's less successful works; it has also been one of the more neglected, even during the present revival of interest in Ovid.[2] There are diminishing returns to be gained from the re-editing of the text, from the investigation of Ovid's sources,[3] and from the study of the chronology of the work;[4] and it is doubtful whether significant progress has been made in these fields in the last twenty years. There has been progress in our understanding of Roman religion and of the calendar, but this has not revealed any unsuspected insights or deficiencies on Ovid's part.[5] It is on the literary side of the *Fasti* that the most interesting work is to be done.

The first obvious question is how far the sceptic of *Ars* 1. 637 has altered his stance in an ostensibly serious work (2. 3 ff., 4. 9 ff.) on Roman religion. The Olympian gods are generally treated with the same kind of detached amusement as in the amatory poems; the spirit of the various divine epiphanies is basically humorous, and such stories as Mars and Minerva (3. 677 ff.) and Priapus and Vesta (6. 319 ff.) do nothing for the majesty of the gods concerned. Here Ovid is following a literary tradition, which has nothing much to do with cult or belief, and the effect of this on the tone of the work as a whole should not be exaggerated. It is also worth pointing out that the *Fasti* is relatively free from the spiteful divine vengeances of the *Metamorphoses* (2. 599 ff. is a rare example), and that Jupiter's love for Callisto (2. 155 ff.) or Europa (5. 605 ff.) is told without the same loss of dignity. But what differentiates the *Fasti* from Ovid's earlier works is not a change of heart towards the Olympian gods, but the broader range of religious experience which the work encompasses, and in particular its treatment of ritual (5. 429 ff.), simple piety (2. 639 ff.), folklore (3. 661 ff.), and what may be called the carnival element (3. 523 ff.). Ovid's role here is that of the perceptive observer (cf. *Am.* 3. 13). The occasional note of friendly scepticism does creep in (2. 45, 2. 551), and there is a certain humour and stylization (4. 747 ff.); but there are also passages of genuine religious feeling, and the total effect is of a sympathetic portrayal of unsophisticated beliefs and customs. As for Ovid's etymologies and aetiological stories, in spite of his claims to be a serious student (1. 7 f., 1. 101) there is no reason to suppose that Ovid had any greater insight into the origins and meanings of the various festivals than had his sources. Where there is a choice of explanations, he is not usually concerned to establish the correct one (1. 332 is an exception); sometimes his aetiological stories, or at least their aetiological import, seem to be his own invention (2. 305 ff., 2. 583 ff., 6. 101 ff.). But the process of syncretism which Roman religion had undergone meant that there was inevitably a gap between the native rite and the imported mythological explanation, and in many cases the true explanation had been confused or lost. Ovid's accounts simply reflect this process of syncretism, and his own inventions can be seen as continuing it.[6]

There is nothing new to say on the astronomical side of the *Fasti*, where Ovid's errors of dating are frequent and notorious.[7] More interesting is the political aspect of the work: in contrast to Ovid's earlier poems, the *Fasti* is full of Augustan propaganda. There are enough indications in the poem of an opposing view to prevent us from taking this Augustanism as sincere. The support of the Augustan cults of Mars (3. 71 ff.) and Venus (4. 19 ff.) has to be taken together with the generally humorous treatment of the Olympian gods; and even Vesta, with whom Augustus was associated as *pontifex maximus*, is made the subject of a coarse Priapus episode. Against the idealized pictures of the rural Rome of Evander (1. 499 ff., 5. 91 ff.) and of the consul summoned from the plough (3. 779 ff.) has to be set Janus' cynical preference for the wealth of the present (1. 223 ff.). The patriotic legends of early Rome are told with an eye more to their literary possibilities than to their patriotic import. The reference to Augustus' moral reforms (2. 139) is overshadowed by stories of coarse lust (1. 393 ff.) and of seduction and abandonment (3. 11 ff., 3. 459 ff.); in the unusual Claudia story (4. 291 ff.) Ovid seems to be making a moral point of his own. On the other hand, this tension is never made so explicit as to be destructive; the Augustan element of the *Metamorphoses* has been taken by some as satirical, but it is difficult to take the same view of the *Fasti.* The fulsomeness of the eulogies does not of itself invite a satirical interpretation;[8] in fact, the references to Augustus as a god already in his lifetime, which are nearly all in connection with the worship of Vesta (1. 530, 3. 421, 4. 954) or the Lares (5. 145), are less extravagant in tone than some of the prophecies of his future godhead in other poets. Nor need we find political significance in Ovid's references to Virgil; in the Anna story (3. 543 ff.) Lavinia is amusingly turned into a jealous shrew and Aeneas' *pietas* is seen in a new light, but this hardly constitutes an attack on the *Aeneid* or on Virgil's political ideals. The final impression is that Ovid's patriotism is not cynical or patently insincere but superficial and perfunctory, designed presumably to rehabilitate the poet in the eyes of the emperor but unrelated to the real purpose of the work. The *Fasti*, like Propertius IV, is a fusion of the Callimachean approach with Roman subject-matter; both are best seen as poetic experiments in developing the Alexandrian tradition (which in fact included panegyric), rather than as genuine political statements of any kind.[9]

Heinze's epoch-making study of Ovid's elegiac narrative technique established some of the main characteristics of the style of the *Fasti,* notably its basically subjective nature, its preference for the gentler emotions (τὸ ἐλεεινόν) over the more violent ones (τὸ δεινόν), and its reduction of the heroic element and of the majesty of the gods. But Heinze exaggerated the differences between the *Fasti* and the *Metamorphoses,* and in pursuing the contrast between elegy and epic he neglected the further comparisons which can be made within elegy itself.[10] For example, Ovid narrates two incidents from the Sabine rape story (*Ars* 1. 101 ff., *Fast.* 3. 179 ff.). In the latter, as Heinze noted, Ovid plays down the heroic and military element to concentrate on the pathos; but he refrains from introducing here the humour and impudence of the *Ars* passage. Similarly, Ovid's account of Hercules and Cacus (*Fast.* 1. 543 ff.) should be compared not only with Virgil's (*Aen.* 8. 184 ff.) but with Propertius' (4. 9). It is true that Ovid omits much of the grandeur and violence of Virgil's account and that his narrative is much less continuous; but he has retained the epic emphasis on the actual Hercules—Cacus fight, whereas Propertius with typical Alexandrian 'asymmetry' concentrates instead on Hercules' subsequent confrontation with the priestess. In these episodes the *Fasti* stands somewhere between the extreme tendencies of epic and those of elegy, and the same might be said for the work as a whole.[11] The diction contains many more echoes of Virgil than might be expected in a non-epic poem; at the same time it contains many echoes of Ovid's amatory works.[12] But in fact the work encompasses so many different genres that it seems unwise to judge the style purely in these terms. It is possible to find in the *Fasti* examples of epic (2. 195 ff.), tragic (6. 587 ff.), comic (3. 675 ff.), elegiac-erotic (3. 11 ff.), bucolic (1. 663 ff.), idyllic (5. 495 ff.), hymn (1. 711 ff.), prayer (4. 747 ff.), fable (2. 247 ff.), novella (1. 393 ff.), and satire (1. 191 ff.); and this immense variety makes stylistic generalization difficult.[13] Some things are fairly constant —the subjectivity of the narrative, the detail and atmosphere of the descriptions, the general verbal dexterity and metrical lightness—but even these need to be studied in relation to individual passages. This has been done for a number of passages; the usual result is to emphasize the versatility and variety of the style.[14]

Related to Heinze's emphasis on the subjective nature of elegy is the concept of the poetic *persona.* This seems indispensable for the appreciation of the *Amores* and helpful for the *Ars*; it is worth asking how relevant it is to the *Fasti*. There are many apparent personal touches in the work, but we may suspect that the personality which emerges is not entirely Ovid's own. He has taken part in some of the rites and festivals (4. 727 ff.), questioned priests or bystanders on others (4. 377 ff., 6. 219 ff.), and on others again has conversed with gods; this last is clearly a poetic fiction, and the others may be, though we cannot exclude some genuine autobiography. He is very conscious of himself as a writer, referring to his researches (1. 289, 1. 657), rebuking himself for foolish mistakes (6. 295), occasionally expressing his own scepticism (2. 551) or guarding against that of his readers (3. 370), and hesitating before telling less salubrious tales (5. 532). He is no detached narrator, but identifies himself with prayers (5. 377), offers comments to his readers (2. 419), and apostrophizes the participants in his stories (2. 811). In this subjective approach Ovid is following the precedents of Callimachus' *Aetia* and Propertius IV, but he seems to develop it further than either.[15] He does not take it as far as in his amatory poems, but for good reason; this approach lends itself very readily to irony, and too much irony would have destroyed the delicate balance maintained in the *Fasti* between wit and seriousness.

One final aspect of the *Fasti* which is due for reappraisal, given current trends in criticism, is the structure of the poem.[16] The decision to follow the calendar imposed severe limitations both on unity and on continuity. There was little Ovid could do towards formal unity, other than the basic unity of subject-matter; and even Ovid's great ingenuity in devising transitions between the many disconnected episodes scarcely turns the *Fasti* into a continuous poem.[17] But he did have some freedom of choice in shaping the individual books and the set-piece episodes, and the structure of these deserves attention. The second book, for example, has elements of formal symmetry in the equidistance of the Cremera and Lucretia episodes from the centre (both episodes of self-sacrifice for an ideal) and in the placing of stories of Romulus' infancy and deification on either side of the centre; and the fact that neither the battle of Cremera nor the deification of Romulus is necessarily dated in February increases the possibility that this symmetry is of Ovid's own making. As for the set-piece episodes, the Lupercalia section of this book is based on a series of interlocking contrasts and similarities of subject-matter and style (Greek and Roman, primitive and sophisticated, plain and elaborate, comic and pathetic); and, if it is true that Ovid himself brought the Hercules–Omphale story into connection with the Lupercalia, this is another case of a deliberately contrived structure. Further studies of this kind might be constructive.[18]

The *Fasti* is the culmination of Ovid's development of elegy; it is the most Callimachean of his elegiac works and also, paradoxically, the most Roman. Its roots in love-elegy are clear enough, in style, in the recurring erotic element (though the Priapus-style burlesque is something new), and in the humorous treatment of the gods; but a new attitude to popular religion has emerged, and Ovid has reversed his previous indifference to the Augustan regime. His range has been widened to embrace a greater variety of themes and styles, and in particular he has brought his elegiac narrative art to its full development. There are many good things in the *Fasti*; yet it is not a satisfying poem to read continuously. The blame is usually laid on Ovid's lack of real sympathy with his subject-matter or on his inability to unite the serious and humorous elements; it might be more perceptive to suggest that his light humour enables him, despite his lack of genuine feeling, to play the role of the patriotic religious poet without hypocrisy or lack of dignity.[19] The comparative failure of the poem as a whole is due rather to formal causes, the discontinuous nature of the calendar and the inability of the elegiac metre to sustain a work of such length. Both of these faults are remedied in the *Metamorphoses*.

Notes

1. There have been recent texts of *Fast.* by F. Bömer, H. Le Bonniec (i Catania, 1969; ii Bologna, 1971), and G. B. Pighi (Turin, 2 vols., 1973); of these Le Bonniec's is the most interesting (Pighi's has been generally criticized for its excessive reliance on G). There has not been a new English translation since Frazer's. Frazer's monumental commentary (London, 5 vols., 1929) is being outdated by advances in anthropological method and in comparative religion; the standard commentary is now Bömer's, which is very thorough on content and (unlike Frazer's) on language. Le Bonniec's Érasme editions of Book I (Paris, 1961; 2nd end. 1965) and Book II (Paris, 1969) can be warmly commended in spite of their small scale; the English-speaking student is still sadly neglected. The best general discussion of *Fast.* is in Bömer's Introduction; see also Santini. F. Peeters, *Les Fastes d'Ovide* (Brussels, 1939), is thorough and still useful, though some of his conclusions (for example, on chronology) cannot be accepted. There is a comprehensive bibliography in Pighi's edition (i. 58 ff.).

2. There is only one *Fasti* article in *Ovidiana*, one in *Atti*, and two in *Wege zu Ovid*; Binns ignores the work completely.

3. On sources and models see Bömer, i. 22 ff. The relevant texts of Varro and Verrius

Flaccus and the other evidence for the Roman calendar are conveniently collected in Pighi's second volume.

4. On the relative chronology of *Fast.* and *Met.* see above (p. 5, with nn. 8 and 9). Books I–VI were completed before Ovid's exile with the rest at most in rough draft (*Tr.* 2. 549 ff.), but there is no means of dating the inception of the work or the separate books. Outside Book I, which was revised after Augustus' death and re-dedicated to Germanicus (1. 3 ff., 1. 285 f., 1. 637 ff.), the latest datable reference is to A.D. 3 (4. 348), though the passage 4. 81 ff. must have been added in exile. On the whole question see Bömer i. 15 ff.

5. See e.g. A. K. Michels, *The Calendar of the Roman Republic* (Princeton, 1967); R. M. Ogilvie, *The Romans and Their Gods in the Age of Augustus* (London, 1969); G. Dumézil, *La Religion romaine archaique* (Paris, 1966; Eng. tr. Chicago, 1970); M. Grant, *Roman Myths* (London, 1971). Citations of Ovid in these studies are not as frequent as commentators on *Fast.* might have led us to expect.

6. On Ovid's treatment of the gods and its literary background see Santini, 48 ff., Frécaut, 275 ff., and G. Lieberg, *Latomus* 28 (1969), 923–47; on Ovid's feeling for rite and common religion see D'Elia, 364 ff., and Frécaut, 283 ff.; on syncretism see R. Schilling, *REL* 46 (1968), 222–35.

7. See Wilkinson, 264 f., and Bömer, i. 28 f.

8. Many of the more extreme passages are in the revised first book, where winning Germanicus' favour is a major objective and satire is unthinkable.

9. For an analysis of Augustan propaganda in *Fast.* see K. Allen, *AJPh* 43 (1922), 250–66; on the 'Einst-Jetzt' motif in Virgil and Ovid see Döpp, 77 ff.; on the failure of Ovid to recapture the spirit of the Roman legends see D'Elia, 327 ff. (Frécaut, 298 ff., is more sympathetic); on the Anna story see Döpp, 56 ff., and Santini, 54 ff.

10. Heinze's whole thesis is subjected to a searching examination by D. A. Little in Zinn, 64–105. On Heinze and *Fast.* see Bömer, i. 44 ff., Otis (2) 23 ff., and Santini, 46 ff. T. F. Brunner, *AJPh* 92 (1971), 275–84, shows that the similes of *Fast.* and *Met.* do conform to the *ἐλεεινόν / δεινόν* distinction.

11. On the Sabine rape episodes see D'Elia, 330 (cf. Heinze, 333 ff.); on Hercules and Cacus see Otis (2), 25 ff.

12. The echoes can be traced in Zingerle, Lüneburg, and Ganzenmüller. On the diction of *Fast.* see also Bömer, i. 49 f., who points to its innovative qualities (prose words, religious terms, new compounds, new *iuncturae*), and suggests that it contains less rhetoric and more pathos than Ovid's amatory elegies.

13. See Kraus (1), 136 ff., and Bömer, i. 47 ff.

14. See e.g. A. G. Lee, *G & R* 23 (1953), 107–18, on Lucretia (cf. Bömer, i. 46 f.); M. von Albrecht, *Wege zu Ovid*, 451–67, on the Chiron episode; R. J. Littlewood, *Latomus* 34 (1975), 1060–72 on the Lupercalia.

15. See further Heinze, 353 ff.; Kraus (1), 133 ff.; Bömer, i. 47; Frécaut, 282 f. As Bömer points out, the figures for apostrophe are much higher in *Fast.* (once in 50 lines) than in *Met.* (once in 120).

16. Compare the negative verdicts of Wilkinson, 268 f., and D'Elia, 342 ff.

17. The variety of Ovid's transitions is illustrated by Bömer, i. 48 f., and Frécaut, 274; D'Elia, 346 f., finds them monotonous.

18. For these two examples see P. Drossart, *IL* 24 (1972), 67–76, and R. J. Littlewood, art. cit.

19. So Frécaut, 300; contrast the unfavourable judgements of Fränkel, 147 ff., and D'Elia, 342 ff.

VI. *METAMORPHOSES*[1]

In contrast to the comparative neglect of the *Fasti*, the *Metamorphoses* has been the subject of several important books and monographs in the last two decades. The most influential of these has been Otis's book *Ovid as an Epic Poet*, which has focused attention on three aspects of the work, its relation to epic, its structure, and its attitude to Augustus.

The discussion of whether the *Metamorphoses* can properly be called an epic has probably outlived its usefulness. The poem satisfies ancient criteria for epic in length (nearly 12,000 lines), metre (hexameters), and to some extent in subject (gods and heroes, if not *reges et proelia*). It does not meet Aristotle's ideas of unity, or have the consistency of tone or seriousness of purpose that are normally associated with epic; it does not even satisfy the criteria laid down by Heinze on the basis of his comparison with the *Fasti*. In particular it is impossible to maintain with Heinze that the gods retain their majesty in the *Metamorphoses* (see, for example, the council of the gods at 1. 163 ff., or the amours of Jupiter and Apollo in Books I and II, or the spiteful vengeances of Diana and Juno in Books III and IV), that the work is based on τὸ δεινόν rather than on τὸ ἐλεεινόν (there is plenty of the latter in the various love-stories, such as Cephalus and Procris or Ceyx and Alcyone), or that the narrative is objective rather than subjective (the *Aeneid* itself has reasonably been called subjective, but there is nothing in it to match the constant intrusion of the author's personality into the *Metamorphoses* with his frequent asides, parentheses, conceits, and other forms of wit).[2] In fact a comparison between the *Aeneid* and the *Metamorphoses* on Heinze's terms would make the latter a very elegiac form of epic. The *Metamorphoses* does have many of the formal elements of epic (set battles, 5. 1 ff., 12. 210 ff.; developed similes, 1. 532 ff., 10. 64 ff.; storms at sea, 11. 474 ff.; catalogues, 2. 217 ff., 3. 206 ff.; descriptions of works of art, 6. 70 ff.; allegorical personifications, 8. 799 ff., 12. 39 ff.); but there is much in it that belongs rather to idyll (8. 618 ff.) or elegy (9. 530 ff., 14. 698 ff.) or bucolic (13. 738 ff.) or didactic (15. 75 ff.). And where the tone and style clearly are epic there is a suspicion that Ovid is merely playing with the conventions; it can be argued that the most serious parts of the *Metamorphoses* are precisely not the epic ones.[3] Hence the descriptions 'epic *sui generis*', 'playful variation of epic', and even 'anti-epic', which have been applied to the work; it is a work of epic proportions which by its very variety defies precise generic classification.

The structure of the poem, with its two hundred and fifty separate stories, is a complex question. The *prooemium* (1. 1–4) suggests a unity based on subject-matter (*in noua mutatas formas corpora*) and a continuity (*perpetuum carmen*) based on the progression from the origins of the world to Ovid's own day. This chronological framework, which is something new to 'collective poetry', seems to have been taken over by Ovid from the universal historians (though there is also a parallel of a sort in Hesiod); at any rate the clear progression from the Creation and Flood (1. 1–451) through the mythological period (1. 452–11. 193) to the historical era of Troy and Rome (11. 194–15. 870) gives the *Metamorphoses* a greater coherence than poems such as Callimachus' *Aetia* or Ovid's own *Fasti.* But in the long mythological section of the poem the chronological system is supplanted by other structural principles. It is difficult to establish the relative chronology of different myths, and Ovid will even reverse the true chronological order when it suits his purposes (for example, in the Theban cycle in Books III and IV). The progress of this section is by no means a simple linear one; techniques such as the story-telling party (4. 36 ff., 5. 294 ff.) and the inset tale-within-a-tale (1. 689 ff., 3. 339 ff.) destroy the chronological sequence and hold up the forward movement. The sense of continuity here thus depends rather on Ovid's ability to link stories into groups and to create ingenious transitions between one story or group of stories and the next. Many of these transitions seem artificial and even arbitrary (2. 533 f., 10. 217 ff.); but there can also be seen in operation a complex system of thematic repetition and contrast which helps to bind the stories together.[4] Some scholars have looked for a formal underlying pattern for this section. Otis sees a thematic forward movement–Divine Comedy (Books I and II), Avenging Gods (3. 1–6. 400), and Pathos of Love (6. 401–11. 795)–with a complicated system of contrasting minor episodes and epic central panels, culminating in the love of Ceyx and Alcyone. Ludwig proposes a symmetrical arrangement of love-sequences and parallel genealogical cycles–Love (1. 452–2. 835), Cadmus (2. 836–4. 606), Perseus (4. 607–5. 249), Love (5. 250–6. 420), Theseus (6. 421–9. 97), Hercules (9. 1–446), and Love (9. 447–11. 193). Both of these proposals have their drawbacks,[5] and the attempt may be misguided: Ovid's treatment of the tapestries of Minerva and Arachne (6. 70 ff.) suggests a preference for fluidity over formally balanced structures. As for the unity of the poem as a whole, metamorphosis, whether or not it is felt to be the real subject of the poem (it is often tangential to or even absent from major stories, such as Phaethon or Meleager), certainly occurs often enough to have a unifying effect. Love, though it does not embrace all aspects of the poem (for example, the philosophical and political parts), is another very prominent, and to that extent unifying, theme. And there are several other minor themes or motifs (such as the search for self-identity or self-fulfilment, divine reward and punishment, the stone and snake motifs, descriptions of landscape) which are prominent in at least some sections of the poem and whose recurrence serves to give the work some unity of texture. In the last analysis the *Metamorphoses* has no single unifying factor; it has a unity of a complex kind, which depends partly on the continuity of the narrative, partly on the multiple repetition of themes, and partly on the personality of the poet, which expresses itself constantly in spite of the diversity of subject-matter and of treatment.[6]

The problem of assessing the political intentions of the *Metamorphoses* has been highlighted by Otis's two changes of mind. In his 1938 article he saw the work as a genuine Augustan epic; in the first edition of his book he posited a conflict between two Ovids, a comic-amatory one and an Augustan one, with the Augustan parts of the poem unsuccessful because basically uncongenial to the poet; and in his second edition he sees even the Augustan parts as deliberate parody or comedy and thus as intentionally anti-Augustan. It seems important to establish how organic to the poem the Augustan element is. It has been argued that the incidental references to Augustus in Book I (176, 204, 562) are intended to create an Augustan 'frame' for the work by anticipating the references in Book XV; if this was the intention it is surprising that the opportunity to strike an Augustan note in the *prooemium* (*ad mea tempora*, 1. 4; cf. *in tua tempora, Tr.* 2. 560) was passed over. Apart from this 'frame' the fact has to be faced that for roughly two-thirds of the poem (Books II to XI) there is practically no Roman reference, and that in the concluding Troy—Rome section the patriotic Roman elements of Virgil's account are reduced to a minimum. Nor is Otis's scheme of epic 'panels' binding together the heroic-Augustan parts of the poem in a continuous development (Phaethon, Perseus, Meleager, and Hercules, leading to the Roman deifications of Aeneas, Romulus, and Caesar) a convincing one. If the *Metamorphoses* has an Augustan plan it can only be in its total movement. Some have seen the creation of cosmos from chaos in Book I as prefiguring the historical progression from chaos to Augustan order, but the whole principle of metamorphosis is one of change rather than order, and the opportunity to emphasize Augustus' restoration of order in Book XV is not really taken (15. 832 ff.). Others, more convincingly, have seen a progression towards Rome as the centre of the civilized world implicit in the movement of the poem from Greece to Rome and especially in the Pythagoras and Aesculapius episodes of Book XV. Whether all this adds up to a conscious Augustan plan may be doubted. If it does, we are forced (with Otis) to choose between genuine (if uncongenial) panegyric and political satire; but it may be that the Augustan plan is illusory, except as a convenient chronological framework with a suitably impressive conclusion.[7]

There can be little doubt that the spirit of the poem as a whole is un-Augustan. The treatment of the gods (including especially Jupiter and Apollo, both figures of Augustan cult) is humorous. The treatment of love, though not as irresponsible as in the *Amores* and *Ars* (in that amid the tales of lust and unnatural passion there are sympathetic accounts of married love), is still unrelated to the Augustan ideal of marriage (contrast the Roman tone of Prop. 4. 11). The golden age of the *Metamorphoses* (1. 89 ff., 15. 96 ff.) has nothing to do with the restored golden age of *Aeneid* 6. 792 f. (or even of *Ars* 3. 113), but is something irrevocably lost in the past. The general treatment of Virgil and the Aeneas-legend is irreverent; apart from using the *Aeneid* as a frame for some essentially unpatriotic tales in the last three books, Ovid has elsewhere mischievously adapted Virgilian themes (for example, the treatment of Juno in Books III and IV, or the allusions to Aeneas and Lavinia in the Perseus–Andromeda episode). And even the Augustan climax is not without its ironies. The inclusion of Rome as the climax of the rise-and-fall-of-cities cycle (15. 418 ff.) throws some doubt on the concept of *Roma aeterna*; the suggestion that Caesar had to be made a god in order that Augustus might be one (15. 760 f.) is an audacious conceit; the picture of Venus touting for the gods' support for the deification of Caesar (15. 761 ff.) is comic; and the prophecy of Augustus' deification (15. 839) is finally overshadowed by Ovid's confident assertion of his own (15. 875 ff.). But there is no need to exaggerate these ironies or to turn the whole poem into a deliberate political statement. What Ovid is doing at the end of the *Metamorphoses* is treating the established order and its own 'mythology' with the same witty irreverence which characterizes most of his work; this does not mean that the poem as a whole is consciously anti-Augustan in any real political sense.[8]

This is not to say that the *Metamorphoses* offers no comment at all on contemporary life. It is possible to see the poem as an escape from contemporary reality into a world of imagination and fantasy, where moral problems are dissolved by metamorphosis and human tragedy is similarly averted; but it is also possible to see it as a reflection of a world of uncertainties and arbitrary force, where the individual has no secure identity and no control over his own destiny.[9] The element of lightness and fantasy in the poem is undeniable and needs no illustration, but the darker element should not be underestimated. Some of the metamorphoses, for example, can only be regarded as unjust and arbitrary and as a destruction of human personality (Callisto, Actaeon, Dryope). There is a good deal of undeserved human suffering, which the metamorphosis endings do not ultimately cancel; physical sufferings in particular are sometimes described in almost sadistic detail (Marsyas, Philomela, Centaurs and Lapiths). The peacefulness of natural settings often turns out to be deceptive and a prelude to violence (Callisto, Proserpina, Scylla).[10] The *melior natura* of the Creation story (1. 21) is soon replaced by lustful or vengeful anthropomorphic gods and eventually by an impersonal system of endless change (15. 176 ff.). The *Metamorphoses* is not in fact based on a coherent philosophical system; the philosophical passages of Books I and XV are coherent neither with each other nor with the main body of the poem, and in particular the Pythagorean system of metempsychosis and continuous change is quite different from the once-for-all metamorphoses of the mythological tales.[11] The metamorphosis theme might have been used to create a cosmos where gods, human beings, animals, and inanimate nature were united by a constant and creative process of interaction and interchange; but the cosmos of Ovid's poem is essentially a man-based world, where the loss of human personality by 'downward' metamorphosis into plants or animals is not compensated for by the occasional 'upward' metamorphosis into stars or gods, or by the 'permanence' which the individual achieves in his new state.[12] But the human interest of the *Metamorphoses* is more psychological than philosophical. A few of the stories involve questions of personal identity, sometimes in direct relation to an actual metamorphosis (Io), but more often not. Here Ovid shows particular sympathy with the uncertainties of the adolescent (Phaethon, Narcissus, Pyramus and

Thisbe); there are also obvious connections with modern psychoanalysis, though we do not need to back-project modern concepts or modern jargon in order to do justice to Ovid's perceptiveness.[13] A great many more stories are concerned with the human experience of love. Here the *Metamorphoses* is remarkable for its wide range (Pyramus and Thisbe, Iphis and Anaxarete, Cephalus and Procris, Ceyx and Alcyone, Baucis and Philemon, Iphis, Pygmalion, Byblis, Myrrha); Ovid has gone far beyond the limited world of love-elegy. In these stories it is not so much a question of psychoanalysis (most of the characters are not especially complex) as of basic human understanding and insight.[14] In this respect the comparison with Ovid's sources, where we can trace them, is illuminating; in several cases (Cephalus and Procris, Iphis, Pygmalion) we can see Ovid creating genuine human feeling which was not present in the pre-existing accounts.[15] This breadth of human sympathy, which is not obscured by the unreality of the atmosphere or by the rhetorical elements in Ovid's style, is one of the outstanding features of the poem.

The style of the *Metamorphoses* is so rich and varied as to make generalization difficult, and adequate illustration is impossible without the detailed examination of extended passages. There is space in this Survey only to refer to some aspects which have been the subject of recent discussion. The essential qualities of Ovid's narrative style are speed and vividness. A lead-in is provided for each story by a swift transition, and little time is wasted on introducing the new characters.[16] The scenic descriptions (*ekphraseis*) with which a number of stories begin contribute both to the vividness of the scene (with their typical pool, wood, cave, and pattern of light and shade) and to the atmosphere, with the apparently tranquil or innocent elements of the setting portending (and even symbolic of) danger or sexuality.[17] The narrative itself can be elliptical and syncopated, even abrupt; details are carefully selected and highlighted in what is almost a cinematic technique.[18] Features which might delay the narrative (such as parenthesis or direct speech) are kept short and carefully integrated into the metrical or syntactical structure.[19] Similes are carefully used to create vividness or emphasize violence and emotion, but are rarely developed at such a length as to distract from the story. The final metamorphosis often comes as an abrupt conclusion, even though its details are described with curious fascination.[20] The verse itself flows smoothly and easily, freed from the jerkiness of the end-stopped elegiac couplet; the reader is carried along by the preponderance of dactyls, the rarity of harsh elisions, the regularity of the caesuras, the co-ordinate sentence structure, and the frequency of enjambment (whole passages can sometimes be read without significant punctuation).[21] The diction is straightforward but never dull; words are coined in moderation and in accordance with established practice, and examples of archaism or vulgarism are rare. The syntax is flexible but not difficult, the most characteristic tendency being towards various forms of hyperbaton and ellipse.[22] But against the classical simplicity of these aspects of style must be set an un-classical exuberance, which produces fanciful descriptions (the flood, the Sun's palace, Phaethon's fall), macabre details (the carnage of Perseus or of Lapiths and Centaurs), exercises in allegory (Envy, Hunger, Sleep, Rumour), lengthy catalogues (Actaeon's hounds, Orpheus' trees), elaborate set speeches (Medea, Ajax–Ulysses, Pythagoras), and so on. Some of these elements are Hellenistic in origin, some the product of rhetorical training, some a reflection of contemporary taste; in their total effect they resemble the mannerist or baroque.[23]

Another important aspect of the style is its pervasive humour.[24] Humour is notoriously difficult to analyse; and perhaps the most useful distinction for the *Metamorphoses* is that made by Cicero (*De Or.* 2. 218 f.) between *dicacitas* and *perpetua festiuitas.* The *dicacitas* of the poem consists of the more superficial kinds of verbal wit, including antithesis, syllepsis, paradox, repetition, and other conceits. The *perpetua festiuitas* is Ovid's good-natured sense of humour, which is implicit in his treatment of his material and often underlined by asides and parentheses; this can be seen especially in his humanization of the gods, in his exploitation of the paradoxes of divine and human behaviour, in his fascination with the incongruous in all its aspects (and especially in the process of metamorphosis), and in his ironic attitude to the credibility of his own stories (10. 28 f., 13. 733 f.). Literary allusion is an important part of the humour of the *Metamorphoses* in both of the above senses, sometimes merely a passing witticism (3. 353 ff.), sometimes implying an ironic attitude to the author or genre in question. Ovid's literary humour is largely based on incongruity and exaggeration (Polyphemus and Galatea, storm of Ceyx) with an element of audacity (as in the basing of Salmacis' speech to Hermaphroditus on that of Odysseus to Nausicaa); these elements are also the basis of his treatment of Virgil, though here there is the added question of his debasement of Virgil's diction by employing it in less solemn contexts and of his deliberate opposition of an Ovidian point of view to Virgil's.[25] That there is an element of parody in Ovid's treatment of other authors is undeniable, but it cannot be claimed that the parody is malicious; Ovid's humour in general is ironic rather than satirical.

The *Metamorphoses* is undoubtedly Ovid's greatest work. Quite apart from the question of scale, it represents the culmination of his narrative and descriptive skills, it shows his creative imagination at its highest, it displays his wit and rhetorical brilliance at its best, and it reveals the full breadth and depth of his understanding of human emotion. It is one of the great works of Roman literature, an achievement which on its own terms challenges comparison with Virgil's *Aeneid*; at the same time in its 'baroque' tendencies it marks the end of the classical era of Roman poetry. It is one of the gains of recent scholarship to have looked beneath the surface of the poem and perceived the complexity of its implications; some have emphasized its element of gaiety and fantasy, some its serious and philosophical aspects, some its psychological insights or satirical intentions. But its essential quality is one which has long been recognized; as Otis says in his latest conclusion, 'When all is said and done, the poet's own humanity comes through.'[26]

Notes

1. The time is ripe for a new critical edition of *Met.* to replace that of Magnus (Berlin, 1914), whose deficiencies are outlined by F. W. Lenz, *Ovid's Metamorphoses: Prolegomena to a Revision of Hugo Magnus' Edition* (Dublin / Zurich, 1967). Editions are forthcoming in the Teubner and O.C.T. series (by Anderson and Tarrant respectively); meanwhile G. M. Edwards's text in Postgate's *Corpus Poetarum Latinorum* (London, 1905) has some claim to be the best available. There is no lack of recent English translations; that by A. E. Watts (Berkeley, 1954) is outstanding, and the versions of M. Innes (Harmondsworth, 1955) in prose and R. Humphries (Bloomington, 1955) and H. Gregory (New York, 1958) in verse all have their merits. The only serviceable commentary on the whole work is the Haupt–Ehwald one (10th edn. Zurich / Dublin, 1966); it is being superseded by that of F. Bömer, which has so far reached Book VII (Heidelberg, i. 1969, ii. 1976, iii. 1977). The English-speaking student is served by the separate editions of A. G. Lee (Book I: Cambridge, 1953), W. S. Anderson (Books VI–X: Norman, 1972), A. S. Hollis (Book VIII: Oxford, 1970), and G. M. H. Murphy (Book XI: London, 1972). The books by Otis and Galinsky provide important general discussions of *Met.*; there are also valuable monographs by von Albrecht, Ludwig, Bernbeck, Segal, and Due. There is a bibliography for *Met.* (from 1914 to 1965) by von Albrecht in his revision of Haupt–Ehwald (i. 457 ff.).

2. On the treatment of the gods see E. Doblhofer, *Philologus* 104 (1960), 69 ff.; Bernbeck, 80 ff.; Frécaut, 246 ff.; and Galinsky, 162 ff. On τὸ ἐλεεινόν see D. A. Little in Zinn, 77 ff. On subjectivity see von Albrecht, *Parenthese,* 189 ff.; Bernbeck, 124 ff.; and Frécaut, 135 ff.

3. So Otis, 366 f. The following quotations are from von Albrecht in Haupt–Ehwald, i. 486; Bernbeck, 130; and Coleman, 475 n. 2. On the whole question see Bernbeck, 123 ff.

4. On Ovid's debt to universal history (and Hesiod) see Ludwig, 74 ff.; on the chronological difficulties of mythology see P. Grimal, *Ovidiana,* 245–57; on the Theban cycle see Otis, 130; on transitions see L. P. Wilkinson, *Ovidiana,* 231–44, and J.-M. Frécaut, *REL* 46 (1968), 247–63; on the combination of linear sequences and inset patterns see Coleman, 463 ff.; on thematic interconnections see Galinsky, 86 ff., and Due, 123 ff.

5. For summaries see Otis, 93, 129, 168, and Ludwig, 55 ff. (cf. Wilkinson, *Ovid Recalled,* 148). Ludwig's symmetry would be more convincing if his sections were all equally cohesive (the Theseus cycle is a very loose one) and of more even lengths.

6. The importance of metamorphosis as the main subject is assumed by Viarre, 39, and Frécaut, 260, but denied by Kenney (2), 146 n. 15, and Galinsky, 3, 97. Otis, 263 f. and *passim,* emphasizes the amatory element. On the snake motif (in the Theban cycle) see F. Norwood, *CJ* 59 (1964), 170–4; on the stone motif (with special reference to Pygmalion) see D. F. Bauer, *TAPhA* 93 (1962), 1–21; on landscape as a unifying theme see Segal (1), 39 ff. M. von Albrecht, *AU* 6 (1963), 47–72 (= *Wege zu Ovid,* 405–37) sees Ovid's humour as important for the unity of the poem.

7. On the Augustan 'frame' and the progression from chaos to cosmos see Ludwig, 82 ff., Döpp, 105 ff., and especially V. Buchheit, *Hermes* 94 (1966), 80–108, who apart from the explicit references in Book I sees Augustan significance in the Jupiter–Lycaon and Apollo–Python episodes and in the war between gods and giants. On epic panels see Otis, 345 and *passim.* On the movement from Greece to Rome see Segal (2), 288 f., and Galinsky, 253. D. A. Little, *Mnemosyne* 25 (1972), 389–401, argues persuasively that the Augustan element is not organic to the poem.

8. The anti-Augustan implications of *Met.* have recently been stressed by Segal (2); W. R. Johnson, *CSCA* 3 (1970), 137 ff.; Coleman, 471 ff.; and Curran, 82 ff. Coleman, 477, and Curran, 90, support the view that *Met.* was a contributory cause of Ovid's banishment (cf. Rand, 92). But the pendulum is swinging back to more moderate views; see Galinsky, 210 ff.; Due, 66 ff.; and D. A. Little, *Prudentia* 8 (1976), 19–35. On the Juno and Perseus episodes see Otis, 131 ff., 159 ff.; on Ovid's treatment of Virgil see further Bernbeck, 117 ff.; Frécaut, 243 ff.; and Galinsky, 217 ff. (Frécaut and Galinsky both minimize the element of parody).

9. The former view is argued strongly by D'Elia, 245 ff., who then has to regard such stories as Myrrha and Byblis as impairing the unity of the poem; for the latter view see Segal (1), 86 ff.

10. On the streak of cruelty in *Met.* see Galinsky, 110 ff.; on violence in a pastoral setting see H. Parry, *TAPhA* 95 (1964), 268–82.

11. So D'Elia, 237 ff.; D. A. Little, *Hermes* 98 (1970), 340–60; and Coleman, 462 f. L. Alfonsi, *Ovidiana,* 265–72, and R. Crahay and J. Hubaux, *Ovidiana,* 283–300, take the Pythagoreanism of Book XV too seriously; on the other hand Segal (2), 278 ff., and W. R. Johnson, *CSCA* 3 (1970), 138 ff., go too far in seeing it as parody (cf. D. A. Little, *Prudentia* 6 (1974), 17–21).

12. On the cosmos of *Met.* see W.-H. Friedrich, *Festschrift für Franz Dornseiff* (Leipzig, 1953), 94–110 (= *Wege zu Ovid,* 362–83), and G. B. Riddehough, *Phoenix* 13 (1959), 201–9, both of whom emphasize the loss of humanity through metamorphosis.

13. The links between modern psychoanalysis and *Met.* are none the less interesting; for discussion and references see Curran, 77 ff., and Galinsky, 45 ff. Curran offers Daphne and Actaeon as examples of a 'false self system' and 'boundary anxiety'. See also Fränkel, 79 ff., on Io and Narcissus; H. Dörrie, *AU* 10 (1967), 54-75, on Narcissus; and Segal (1), 49 ff., on Pyramus and Thisbe. For other modern aspects of Ovid's psychology see Viarre, 388 ff.

14. On Ovid's portrayal of love see D'Elia, 255 ff.; Otis, 263 ff. (who emphasizes the idealization of conjugal love); and R. W. Garson, *Prudentia* 8 (1976), 9–18 (who illustrates the variety of situation and treatment).

15. See Otis's useful Appendix (375 ff.). The discussions of Ovid's sources by Lafaye and Castiglioni are still basic (with von Albrecht's important introduction to the 1971 reprint of Lafaye). For a recent account of Ovid's sources and models see Due, 15 ff.

16. So Bernbeck, 44 ff.

17. On the symbolic element see Segal (1). The question of Ovid's debt to contemporary wall-painting and to other forms of classical art is still debated (see esp. Viarre, 45 ff.). It seems highly probable that Ovid's imagination was stimulated by works of visual art, but direct influence on *Met.* can be seen in relatively few cases (see the negative conclusions of H. Herter, *Ovidiana,* 49–74). This is a separate question from the common

tendencies of *Met.* and contemporary art in matters such as fluidity of structure or realism / fantasy; on these see Bernbeck, 135 ff., and Galinsky, 83 ff.

18. On syncopation and abruptness see R. Crahay, *Atti* i. 91 ff., and Bernbeck, 1 ff.; on cinematic techniques see Viarre, 100 ff.

19. On parenthesis see von Albrecht, *Parenthese*, esp. 26 ff.; on direct speech see J. Marouzeau, *Ovidiana*, 101–5.

20. On similes see J. Richardson, *CJ* 59 (1964), 161–9, and T. F. Brunner, *CJ* 61 (1966), 354–63 (cf. Washietl, Owen, and Wilkins); on the metamorphosis descriptions see Kenney (2), 142 ff., who comments on their intellectual rather than human qualities.

21. On Ovid's versification see Lee's edition of *Met.* I, 31 ff.; G. Duckworth, *Vergil and Classical Hexameter Poetry* (Michigan, 1969), 71 ff.; Kenney (2), 119, 135 ff.; Anderson's edition of *Met.* VI–X, 24 ff.; and W. Ott, *Metrische Analysen zu Ovid Metamorphosen Buch I* (Tübingen, 1974).

22. On diction and syntax see Kenney (2), 120 ff., 128 ff.

23. On the 'baroque' element see Wilkinson, 155 ff.; D'Elia, 300 ff.; H. Bardon, *Ovidiana,* 82 ff.; R. Crahay, *Atti* i. 91–110.

24. See the studies of E. Doblhofer, *Philologus* 104 (1960), 63–91; M. von Albrecht, *AU* 6 (1963), 47–72 (= *Wege zu Ovid,* 405–37); and Galinsky, 158 ff. The whole subject is well illustrated by Frécaut (esp. 27 ff., 114 ff., 135 ff., 237 ff.).

25. See F. Bömer, *Gymnasium* 66 (1959), 268–87 (= *Wege zu Ovid,* 173–202), and R. Lamacchia, *Maia* 12 (1960), 310–30.

26. See Otis, 374.

VII. *TRISTIA* AND *EX PONTO*[1]

The letters from exile have been the least appreciated and most heavily criticized of Ovid's works. In the past scholars found interest in details of biography, prosopography, chronology, and ethnography; but in general they were very ready to accept Ovid's own view of the poetry as monotonous, repetitious, and of inferior quality (*Pont.* 1. 5, 3. 9), and to add their own condemnation of the servile flattery used by the poet in his efforts to secure a better fate. More recently Ovid's attitude to Augustus has been re-examined to suggest considerable independence of spirit, and a careful examination of individual elegies has revealed a richer poetic quality than had generally been suspected.

We may deal first with the major biographical question, the causes of Ovid's exile (*carmen et error, Tr.* 2. 207).[2] There is no doubt that the *carmen* was the *Ars Amatoria*; but in spite of continuing discussion of the *error*, it seems increasingly unlikely that we shall ever be able to uncover what it was. The two most popular theories are still those which connect Ovid with the sexual misconduct of the younger Julia (exiled in A.D. 8, the year of Ovid's banishment) or with the dynastic rivalries of the Julio-Claudian family. In either case it is clear that Ovid was involved only incidentally; in brief, he had inadvertently witnessed a crime (*Tr.* 2. 103 ff.). If the affair was purely a sexual scandal, it is strange that D. Silanus, the lover of Julia, was punished less harshly than Ovid. In this case it would seem to follow that the *carmen* was the real cause and the *error* merely a pretext; Ovid certainly emphasizes the *carmen* in *Tristia* II and elsewhere, but this may be because this was the easier charge to refute in public (*Pont.* 2. 9. 75 f.). In favour of the political explanation is the possible connection of Ovid with Agrippa Postumus (exiled A.D. 7) through Fabius Maximus (*Pont.* 4. 6. 9 ff.; cf. Tac. *Ann.* 1. 5) and the fact that after Augustus' death Tiberius maintained the same hostility towards Ovid's pleas. It seems worth emphasizing that at the time Augustus was in a politically vulnerable situation through military, financial, and dynastic difficulties;[3] this must have been the prime reason for the harshness of Ovid's sentence. On the other hand it is hard to believe that Ovid was actually part of any political plot, and his real crime in Augustus' eyes must have been the attack implied in his poetry on the emperor's moral programme.

The *Tristia* and *Ex Ponto* are not personal poetry in any simple sense of the term. Ovid's private correspondence from exile was carried out in prose (*Pont.* 4. 2. 5 f.); poetry is never private, and even the letters addressed to particular recipients are evidently intended for a wider audience. But the letters from exile, unlike much other Latin 'personal poetry', are firmly grounded in a real-life situation; the *ego* in these poems is essentially Ovid, not some adopted *persona.* Herein lies one of the fascinations of the *Tristia* and *Ex Ponto*; and we should not let the literary critic's aversion to autobiographical approaches blind us to the real interest of these poems as human documents.[4] The fact that they have a practical purpose—namely to secure some improvement in Ovid's sentence—gives them added interest, though it also means that we cannot take them at face value; in his descriptions of the rigours of Tomis or of his own poetic incapacity or even of the ultimate friendliness of the local inhabitants, Ovid may well be exaggeratin' in order to increase the sympathy and indignation and even sense of guilt of his readers. But the outline of the picture must be true; and the fact that the various books have come down to us more or less in order of composition[5] enables us to trace the gradual development of Ovid's attitudes. Three interesting aspects are his hopes of a change of sentence (cf. *Tr.* 1. 1. 34, *Tr.* 3. 5. 53 f., and *Pont.* 3. 7. 19), his attitude towards the native inhabitants (cf. *Tr.* 5. 7. 9 ff. and *Pont.* 4. 14. 47 ff.), and his feelings towards his wife (cf. *Tr.* 3. 3 and *Pont.* 3. 1). Most interesting of all is his attitude towards the poems which he is writing. At first his apologies for their quality are little more than conventional (*Tr.* 1. 1. 35 ff.) or at least reasonable statements of the difficulties of composition in a foreign land with no books or audience to stimulate or friends to help or criticize (*Tr.* 3. 14. 27 ff.). But in the later books there is an increasing insistence that he no longer writes to gain fame or to exercise his poetic talent (*Tr.* 5. 1. 27, 5. 1. 75); he shirks the now irksome task of correcting his own work (*Pont.* 1. 5. 17 ff.); he writes because he cannot help it (*Tr.* 5. 12. 59 f.), though writing is no longer easy and gives him no pleasure (*Pont.* 4. 2. 25 ff.).[6] At the same time he never quite loses sight of the sacred calling of the poet (*Tr.* 4. 1. 29, *Pont.* 3. 4. 89); his poetry is a reward for his friends (*Pont.* 2. 6. 33 f.), a consolation to himself (*Pont.* 4. 16. 2 f.), and a threat to his enemies (*Tr.* 4. 9. 26).

Ovid's major enemy was of course Augustus himself, though he could not be directly represented as such. There is a large amount of abject flattery in the exile poetry, both of Augustus and later of Tiberius, Livia, and Germanicus; but the most extreme examples are in the later books (*Tr.* 5. 2. 45 ff., *Pont.* 2. 8), and behind the earlier adulation of Augustus there is a good deal of implied criticism.[7] *Tristia* II is a good example. Though ostensibly addressed to Augustus as a plea for leniency, it in fact contains much that is critical and even impudent: Augustus has treated Ovid more cruelly than any *hostis* (43 ff.) and has banished him further from his native land than any other exile (187 ff.); he had given no indication of disapproval of Ovid in the annual reviews of the *equites* (89 ff.) and had not punished the *Ars* at the time of its publication (545 f.); being occupied with military problems and moral reforms (two touchy matters!) he has not had time to read the *Ars* himself or evaluate its real purpose or effects (213 ff.); he had not punished other love-poets (361 ff.) or even those who gave instructions for dice-playing (illegal at Rome but a favourite pastime of the emperor himself) (471 ff.); he has himself put on mime shows which were far more indecent than anything written by Ovid (497 ff.). There is much to be said for the view that the poem is an appeal over the head of Augustus to Ovid's friends and to the wider literary public of Rome, designed to show the arbitrariness of Augustus' treatment of Ovid. The same is true of the exile poems as a whole. Ovid's frequent admissions that his punishment is deserved (indeed Augustus has been merciful in sparing Ovid's life) (*Tr.* 1. 1. 20) are balanced by equally frequent assertions that he has committed no crime (*Tr.* 1. 2. 95 ff.). The repeated references to Augustus' clemency, if not openly casting doubt on the emperor's possession of that virtue, at least emphasize his unreasonableness in not extending it to Ovid (*Tr.* 5. 2. 35 ff.). Even the identification with Jupiter, which is a major form of Ovid's flattery of Augustus, is accompanied by the notion that Augustus' anger should not exceed Jupiter's (*Tr.* 2. 33 ff.). The *pax Augusta* is mentioned only to make the point that it is denied to Ovid (*Pont.* 2. 7. 67 f.); Augustus may have won the *corona ciuilis*, but his saving of citizens does not extend to Ovid (*Tr.* 3. 1. 47 ff.). Ovid expresses regret at having written the *Ars* (*Tr.* 5. 12. 67 f.), but, significantly, it is as *tenerorum lusor amorum* that he wishes to be remembered in both his epitaph and his autobiography (*Tr.* 3. 3. 73, 4. 10. 1). The most defiant passage of all is that which proclaims that Augustus has no power over Ovid's poetic talent (*Tr.* 3. 7. 45 ff.); he cannot destroy his fame, and he cannot prevent him being read. The writing of poetry was basic to Ovid's whole life, and this is a point which for all his flattery and self-abasement he never conceded.

But the autobiographical approach has its limitations, and recent scholarship has rightly concentrated on the much neglected literary aspects of the exile poems. In the *Tristia* and *Ex Ponto* Ovid was responding not only to the situation of an exile but to the challenge of making poetry out of that situation, which in itself implies a certain distancing from autobiographical 'fact'. In creating a poetry of exile, Ovid had few, if any, models to follow (Alcaeus is a possible forerunner, but it seems unlikely that Ovid used him); and the originality of the enterprise deserves to be underlined. Cicero's letters from exile provided a possible prose precedent. In fact there are a number of striking parallels between these and Ovid's exile poems (*Att.* 3. 7. 2 / *Pont.* 1. 9. 21 f.; *Att.* 3. 8. 4 / *Pont.* 1. 1. 61); these would suggest, if we could prove deliberate imitation, that Ovid was aiming to enshrine in his poetry not merely his own experience but the typical reactions of the exile.[8] As for the form of the verse epistle, there were two recent precedents. Horace's *Epistles* were, like Ovid's, autobiographical in essence, and even included a letter to Augustus (*Ep.* 2. 1 / *Tr.* 2). But Horace's *Epistles* are much more reflective and philosophical than Ovid's, and such allusions as Ovid makes (*Tr.* 1. 1. / *Ep.* 1. 20; *Pont.* 1. 5. 19 f. / *Ars. P.* 291) scarcely warrant the assumption that Ovid saw himself as following in Horace's footsteps.[9] The *Heroides* are a much closer parallel, both in metre (elegiacs) and in subject-matter (lament). There is obviously a sense in which the exile poems are an adaptation of the *Heroides*; the laments of heroines separated from their lovers have become the laments of the poet separated from his fatherland and friends, and in setting his own situation against that of the heroines, Ovid is again to some extent universalizing his experience. There are some obvious cross-references from the exile poems to the *Heroides*; Ovid's departure from Rome (*Tr.* 1. 3) has several motifs in common with the departure scenes in the *Heroides*, his instructions for his own epitaph (*Tr.* 3. 3. 73 ff.) recall those of several of the heroines, and the occasional epistolary conceits have their counterparts in the earlier collection (*Tr.* 5. 13. 1 f. / *Her.* 4. 1 f.).[10] But the differences are still considerable. Instead of a series of mythological situations, where Ovid could on the basis of pre-existing versions practise the art of *uariatio* in matters of character, setting, and treatment, there is now a single real-life situation, which presents unique poetic problems of its own. The exile poetry has been called 'a series of poetic experiments';[11] it is, in effect, a new genre.

The poems of the *Tristia* and *Ex Ponto* which have been most valued have tended to be those with the most direct appeal, either as pieces of narrative or description or as expressions of simple emotion (despair, *Tr.* 3. 3; pride, *Tr.* 3. 7; nostalgia, *Tr.* 3. 12; love *Tr.* 4. 3; resignation, *Pont.* 3. 7). Others have been undervalued because sufficient attention has not been paid to their less obvious poetic qualities. There is space here only to indicate a few fruitful approaches. The pieces of description are not simply literal; they are literary and often also symbolic. The storm in *Tristia* 1. 2 has echoes of the storm of Ceyx in *Metamorphoses* XI; it is also symbolic of the shipwreck of Ovid's fortunes (*Tr.* 1. 5. 36). The departure poem (*Tr.* 1. 3) has allusions to motifs from the *Heroides* and to the fall of Troy; its death imagery is symbolic of exile as death (*Tr.* 1. 4. 28). The description of Tomis (*Tr.* 3. 10) makes use of Virgil's description of Scythia in *Georgics* III; the barrenness of the climate is obviously symbolic of the hopelessness of Ovid's situation.[12] Literary allusion is in fact ubiquitous—chiefly to Catullus, Horace, Virgil, and Ovid's own earlier works—and to ignore it is often to miss the point of what Ovid is doing. Sometimes it is a mere passing reference which enriches by its associations (*Tr.* 3. 8. 29 f. / V. *Aen.* 6. 309 ff.); sometimes it is a device for presenting a familiar point in a new and significant way (*Pont.* 3. 3. 5 ff. / *Rem.* 549 ff.); often there is an underlying irony in the reversal of the happier situation in the model (*Tr.* 1. 10 / Cat. 4). In particular many of the themes (and much of the vocabulary) of love-elegy reappear in a new guise. This kind of irony of reversal had always been a feature of Ovid's work, but now it gains a new seriousness, and even bitterness, in its application to the poet's own situation.[13] Mythology too gains a new seriousness, not the witty incongruities of the love-poems, nor the wide-ranging imaginative re-creations of the *Metamorphoses,* but a limited number of *exempla* recurring like leitmotifs to emphasize the essence of Ovid's position (Ulysses and Jason for Ovid's sufferings; Penelope and Andromache for his wife's devotion; Theseus and Pirithous, Orestes and Pylades, Achilles and Patroclus, Nisus and Euryalus for the loyalty of his friends; Busiris, Phalaris, and Perillus for the cruelty of his tormentors). These mythological parallels may serve to magnify Ovid's sufferings, but in the end myth is acknowledged to be an illusion. Ovid may desire to imitate mythological characters in winged flight (*Tr.* 3. 8. 1 ff.) or in metamorphosis (*Pont.* 1. 2. 29 ff.), but the grim reality is that he cannot.[14] Finally, the structure of the separate books. In spite of Ovid's claim (*Pont.* 3. 9. 51 ff.) to have collected the Pontic letters into books *sine ordine,* it is clear that the exile books were in fact carefully arranged compositions. The books of the *Tristia* are arranged on a basis of variety and symmetry (if not with the perfect symmetry which some critics would like to find); the first three Pontic books have a symmetrical arrangement by addressee.[15] And this is not merely a matter of aesthetics. The importance often given to the central poem of a book justifies a careful look at poems in this position: for example, *Tristia* 1. 6, in praise of Ovid's wife, has a wider significance as a statement of the power of poetry.[16]

In short, though there is no need to exaggerate the merits of the exile poetry, its human interest is undeniable, and its alleged monotony begins to disappear when the individual poems are carefully examined from a literary aspect.[17]

Notes

1. There are recent texts of *Tr.* and *Pont.* by G. Luck (Zurich, 1963) and in the Budé series by J. André (*Tr.*: Paris, 1968; *Pont.*: Paris, 1977). The exile poems lack major commentaries. Luck's *Tr.* commentary (Heidelberg, i. 1967; ii. 1968 and 1972) has so far reached Book II; meanwhile S. G. Owen's edition of *Tr.* II (Oxford, 1924) has been reprinted (Amsterdam, 1967). For other books we have to turn to the doctoral dissertations of T. J. de Jonge (*Tr.* IV: Groningen, 1951), J. T. Bakker (*Tr.* V: Amsterdam, 1946), and U. Staffhorst (*Pont.* III. 1–3: Würzburg, 1965). A. L. Wheeler's Loeb edition (London, 1924) has a useful introduction and index; there is a more recent English translation by L. R. Lind (Athens, 1975). The only full-length discussion of the exile poems is that of Frösch, who also provides a full and up-to-date bibliography (187 ff.).

2. The whole question is thoroughly discussed by J. C. Thibault, *The Mystery of Ovid's Exile* (Berkeley, 1964), who is unable to reach any positive conclusion. See also André's *Tr.* edition (vii ff.), who inclines to a political explanation, and F. Norwood, *CPh* 58 (1963), 150–63, who ingeniously combines the sexual and political aspects.

3. See D'Elia, 371 ff., and T. Wiedemann, *CQ* 25 (1975), 264–71.

4. For a sympathetic biographical approach see Fränkel, 117 ff., 155 ff., and Wilkinson, 285 ff., 322 ff.; and, more recently, Y. Bouynot, *Atti* i. 249–68, and W. Willige, *AU* 12 (1969), 51–72.

5. The dates are: *Tr.* I, A.D. 8–9; *Tr.* II, A.D. 9; *Tr.* III, A.D. 9–10; *Tr.* IV, A.D. 10–11; *Tr.* V, A.D. 11–12; *Pont.* I–III (a single collection), A.D. 12–13; *Pont.* IV, A.D. 13–16. For the possibility that some of the letters of *Pont.* I–III were actually written earlier see H. B. Evans, *Hermes* 104 (1976), 103–12. On the whole question see Wheeler's Loeb Introduction (xxxiii ff.).

6. For scepticism on the truth of these claims see Frösch, 73 ff. G. Luck, *HSPh* 65 (1961), 243–61, shows by an examination of various linguistic features that there is no technical decline in the exile poetry.

7. There are important discussions by R. Marache, *Ovidiana,* 412–19, and W. Marg, *Atti* ii. 345–54 (= *Wege zu Ovid,* 502–12). See also N. I. Herescu, *Ovidiana,* 420–42, and N. Voulikh, *LEC* 36 (1968), 370–82.

8. So Frösch, 77 ff. On Ovid and Cicero see also D'Elia, 386 ff. There are many other parallels not specifically noted by either, as a reading of *Att.* III (*passim*), *Fam.* XIV (esp. 1–4), and *Q. Fr.* 1. 3 will reveal. The problem of deliberate imitation is complicated by the uncertainty of the date of publication of *Fam.,* which may not have been before Neronian times.

9. On Ovid and Horace see Rahn, 480 ff., who goes too far in ascribing a 'legitimizing' aim to Ovid's allusions to Horace and in seeing an attempt by Ovid to take over Horace's role as literary correspondent to Augustus.

10. On the links with *Her.* see Rahn, 479 f., 484 ff.

11. So Kenney (3), 38.

12. On *Tr.* 1. 2 and 1. 3 see Dickinson, 161 ff., and Frösch, 25 ff.; on *Tr.* 3. 10 see S. Besslich, *Gymnasium* 79 (1972), 177–91.

13. For further examples see Zingerle, Lüneburg, and Ganzenmüller. There is an excellent discussion of this aspect of the exile poetry by Kenney (3); see also A. G. Lee, *G & R* 18 (1949), 113–20, on *Tr.* 3. 8. For the reversal of themes see also Wimmel, 297 ff., on the *recusatio*; G. K. Galinsky, *WSt* 82 (1969), 102–7, on the triumph; Stroh, 250 ff., on wooing through poetry; F. Cairns, *Generic Composition in Greek and Roman Poetry* (Edinburgh, 1972), 135 ff., on the birthday poem.

14. On myth in the exile poems see Frécaut, 317 ff.; on the significance of the Ulysses role see Rahn, 493 ff.

15. The possibilities, and limitations, of book-analysis are indicated by Dickinson's discussion of *Tr.* On *Pont.* I–III see H. H. Frösch, *Ovids Epistulae ex Ponto I–III als Gedichtsammlung* (Diss. Bonn, 1968), who implausibly proposes to transpose 2. 11 to follow 3. 4 to produce perfect symmetry (136 ff.). *Pont.* IV, which was published posthumously, has no clear structure.

16. On the central position see Port, 457 ff.; on *Tr.* 1. 6 see Kenney (3), 39 ff.

17. See further the studies of *Pont.* 1. 4 and 3. 6 by J. Benedum, *Studien zur Dichtkunst des späten Ovid* (Diss. Giesen, 1967), 8 ff., 65 ff.

APPENDIX OF PRINCIPAL REFERENCES

ALBRECHT, M. VON, *Die Parenthese in Ovids Metamorphosen und ihre dichterische Funktion* (Hildesheim, 1964).

ANDERSON, W. S., 'The *Heroides*' in Binns, *Ovid*, 49–83.

Atti del convegno internazionale ovidiano, Sulmona 1958 (Rome, 2 vols, 1959).

AXELSON, B., *Unpoetische Wörter* (Lund, 1945).

BERNBECK, E. J., *Beobachtungen zur Darstellungsart in Ovids Metamorphosen* (Munich, 1967).

BINNS, J. W. (ed.), *Ovid* (Classical Literature and its Influence) (London, 1973).

BÖMER, F. (ed.), *Ovid: die Fasten* (Heidelberg, 2 vols, 1957–8).

CASTIGLIONI, L., *Studi intorno alle fonti e alla composizione delle Metamorfosi di Ovidio* (Pisa, 1906; repr. Rome, 1964).

COLEMAN, R. 'Structure and Intention in the *Metamorphoses*', *CQ* 21 (1971), 461–77.

CURRAN, L. C., 'Transformation and Anti-Augustanism in Ovid's *Metamorphoses*', *Arethusa* 5 (1972), 71–91.

D'ELIA, S., *Ovidio* (Naples, 1959).

DE SAINT DENIS, E., 'Le malicieux Ovide', *Ovidiana*, 184–200.

DICKINSON, R. J., 'The *Tristia*: Poetry in Exile' in Binns, *Ovid*, 154–90.

DÖPP, S., *Virgilischer Einfluss im Werk Ovids* (Munich, 1968).

DÖRRIE, H., 'Die dichterische Absicht Ovids in den *Epistulae Heroidum*', *A&A* 13 (1967), 41–55.

DUE, O. S., *Changing Forms: Studies in the Metamorphoses of Ovid* (Copenhagen, 1974).

DU QUESNAY, I. M. LE M., 'The *Amores*' in Binns, *Ovid*, 1–48.

FRÄNKEL, H., *Ovid: a Poet Between Two Worlds* (Berkeley, 1945; repr. 1956).

FRÉCAUT, J.-M., *L'Esprit et l'humour chez Ovide* (Grenoble, 1972).

FRÖSCH, H. H., *Ovid als Dichter des Exils* (Bonn, 1976).

GALINSKY, G. K., *Ovid's Metamorphoses: an Introduction to the Basic Aspects* (Oxford, 1975).

GANZENMÜLLER, C., 'Aus Ovids Werkstatt', *Philologus* 70 (1911), 274–311, 397–437.

HEINZE, R., 'Ovids elegische Erzählung', *Berichte der sächsischen Akademie zu Leipzig* 71 (1919); repr. in *Vom Geist des Römertums* (Darmstadt, 4th edn. 1972), 308-403. References are to the latter.

HOLLIS, A. S., 'The *Ars Amatoria* and *Remedia Amoris*' in Binns, *Ovid*, 84–115.

JACOBSON, H., *Ovid's Heroides* (Princeton, 1974).

KENNEY, E. J. (1), 'Nequitiae poeta', *Ovidiana*, 201–9.

– – (2), 'The Style of the *Metamorphoses*' in Binns, *Ovid*, 116–53.

– – (3), 'The Poetry of Ovid's Exile', *PCPhS* 11 (1965), 37–49.

KRAUS, W. (1), 'Ovidius Naso', *RE* 18 (1942), 1910–86; repr. in *Wege zu Ovid*, 67–166. References are to the latter.

– – (2), 'Die Briefpaare in Ovids Heroiden', *WSt* 65 (1950), 54–77; repr. in *Wege zu Ovid*, 269–94. References are to the latter.

LAFAYE, G., *Les Métamorphoses d'Ovide et leurs modèles grecs* (Paris, 1904; repr. Hildesheim, 1971).

LEACH, E. W., 'Georgic Imagery in the *Ars Amatoria*', *TAPhA* 95 (1964), 142–54.

LEE, A. G., 'Tenerorum Lusor Amorum' in J. P. Sullivan (ed.), *Critical Essays on Roman Literature: Elegy and Lyric* (London, 1962), 149–79.

LINSE, E., *De P. Ovidio Nasone Vocabulorum Inventore* (Leipzig, 1891).

LUDWIG, W., *Struktur und Einheit der Metamorphosen Ovids* (Berlin, 1965).

LÜNEBURG, A., *De Ovidio Sui Imitatore* (Diss. Jena, 1888).
MARG, W., 'Ovids Amores: Dichter und Dichtung', *Wege zu Ovid,* 295–312.
OPPEL, E., *Ovids Heroides: Studien zur inneren Form und zur Motivation* (Diss. Erlangen–Nürnberg, 1968).
OTIS, B. (1), 'Ovid and the Augustans', *TAPhA* 69 (1938), 188–229.
– – (2), *Ovid as an Epic Poet* (Cambridge, 1966; 2nd edn. 1970).
Ovidiana: Recherches sur Ovide (ed. Herescu, N. I.) (Paris, 1958).
OWEN, S. G., 'Ovid's Use of the Simile', *CR* 45 (1931), 97–106.
PLATNAUER, M., *Latin Elegiac Verse* (Cambridge, 1951; repr. Hamden, 1971).
PORT, W., 'Die Anordnung in Gedichtbüchern augusteischer Zeit', *Philologus* 81 (1926), 280–308, 427–68.
RAHN, H., 'Ovids elegische Epistel', *A&A* 7 (1958), 105–20; repr. in *Wege zu Ovid,* 476–501. References are to the latter.
RAND, E. K., *Ovid and His Influence* (Boston, 1925; repr. New York, 1963).
REITZENSTEIN, E., 'Das neue Kunstwollen in den Amores Ovids', *RhM* 84 (1935), 62–86; repr. in *Wege zu Ovid,* 206–32. References are to the latter.
RUDD, N., *Lines of Enquiry: Studies in Latin Poetry* (Cambridge, 1976).
SANTINI, C., 'Toni e strutture nella representazione delle divinità nei Fasti', *GIF* 25 (1973), 41–62.
SEGAL, C. P. (1), *Landscape in Ovid's Metamorphoses: a Study in the Transformations of a Literary Symbol* (Wiesbaden, 1969).
– – (2), 'Myth and Philosophy in the *Metamorphoses*: Ovid's Augustanism and the Augustan Conclusion of Book XV', *AJPh* 90 (1969), 257–92.
STÖSSL, F. *Ovid: Dichter und Mensch* (Berlin, 1959).
STROH, W., *Die römische Liebeselegie als werbende Dichtung* (Amsterdam, 1971).
Studi Ovidiani (Rome, 1959).
VIARRE, S., *L'Image et la pensée dans les Métamorphoses d'Ovide* (Paris, 1964).
WASHIETL, J. A., *De Similitudinibus Imaginibusque Ovidianis* (Vienna, 1883).
Wege zu Ovid = Albrecht, M. von and Zinn E. (eds.), *Ovid* (Wege der Forschung 92) (Darmstadt, 1968).
WILKINS, E. G., 'A Classification of the Similes of Ovid', *CW* 25 (1932), 73–8, 81–6.
WILKINSON, L. P., *Ovid Recalled* (Cambridge, 1955).
WILLIAMS, G., *Tradition and Originality in Roman Poetry* (Oxford, 1968).
WIMMEL, W., *Kallimachos in Rom* (Wiesbaden, 1960).
ZINGERLE, A., *Ovidius und sein Verhältnis zu den vorgängern und gleichzeitigen römischen Dichtern* (Innsbruck, 3 vols, 1869–71; repr. Hildesheim, 1967).
ZINN, E. (ed.), *Ovids Ars amatoria und Remedia amoris: Untersuchungen zum Aufbau* (Stuttgart, 1970).